FAITHFUL CITIZENS

FAITHFUL CITIZENS

A Practical guide to Catholic Social Teaching and Community Organising

Austen Ivereigh

DARTON · LONGMAN + TODD

First published in 2010 by
Darton, Longman and Todd Ltd
1 Spencer Court
140 – 142 Wandsworth High Street
London SW18 4JJ

ISBN 978-0-232-52789-6

A catalogue record for this book is available from the British Library.

Phototypeset by Kerrypress Ltd, Luton, Bedfordshire.
Printed and bound in Great Britain by Cromwell Press Group, Trowbridge, Wiltshire.

For L, who made this possible

CONTENTS

ACKNOWLEDGEMENTS

Neil Jameson, London Citizens lead organiser, gave me the time out to do this, and my energetic and inspiring West London Citizens organiser colleagues – Julie Camacho, Marzena Cichon, Jonny Scott and Jessica Kennedy – bore the brunt of my absences. Many leaders and organisers in London Citizens, especially Bernadette Farrell, shared their stories, and inspired me by their commitment and skill. Three citizen-theologian academics – Angus Ritchie, Luke Bretherton and Maurice Glasman – shaped many of the thoughts in these pages. London Citizens trustees graciously backed the project, and Jonathan Lange of the Industrial Areas Foundation opened up the wider world of organising. Catherine Howarth, first West London Citizens organiser, wrote important sections of Chapter 4. Brendan Walsh and his team at Darton, Longman & Todd were a delight to deal with. To you all, a big thank you.

LIST OF ABBREVIATIONS

The following abbreviations have been used in references.

CA	*Centesimus Annus*
CCC	*Catechism of the Catholic Church*
CSDC	*Compendium of the Social Doctrine of the Church*
CV	*Caritas in Veritate*
DCE	*Deus Caritas Est*
EJ	*Economic Justice for All* (US bishops' letter)
EMCC	*Erga Migrantes Caritas Christi*
GS	*Gaudium et Spes*
JM	*Justitia in Mundo*
LE	*Laborem Exercens*
MM	*Mater et Magistra*
OA	*Octogesima Adveniens*
PP	*Populorum Progressio*
PT	*Pacem in Terris*
QA	*Quadragesimo Anno*
RN	*Rerum Novarum*
SRS	*Sollicitudo Rei Socialis*

INTRODUCTION

It belongs to the layperson, without waiting passively for orders and directives, to take the initiative freely and to infuse a Christian spirit into the mentality, customs, laws and structures of the community in which they live.

Pope Paul VI (*PP* 81)

If the Catholic Church is not today the dominant social dynamic force, it is because Catholic scholars have taken the dynamite of the Church, have wrapped it up in nice phraseology, placed it in a hermetic container and sat on the lid. It is time to blow the lid off so the Catholic Church may again be the dominant social dynamic force.

Dorothy Day[1]

Faithful Citizens blows the lid off the container of Catholic social teaching. It shows how ordinary Catholics, working with ordinary people of other and no faiths for the common good, bring about concrete gains for the less well-off in society, while building the power of civil society to hold the state and the market to account.

It's the story of how London Citizens' 150 member organisations, mostly faith-based, more than a third of them Catholic parishes and schools, translate the principles of Catholic social teaching (CST) into action, not just in the justice they pursue, but in the way they pursue it – by strengthening solidarity, or civic friendship, through community organising's 'relational' approach to politics.

It's the story of a certain kind of politics with its roots in Depression-era Chicago, the kind of politics which the popes call for. We might call it 'citizen politics', or 'civil-society' politics. Let me explain.

Most Christians believe that they have a duty to the poor, primarily through direct assistance to the needy. Others believe that the Church must play its part in bringing about a more just world, because personal acts of charity do not suffice to meet the demands of justice.

But in his recent encyclical letter *Caritas in Veritate* (*CV*), Pope Benedict XVI rejects these as alternatives. Justice and charity need each other. They are part of the same thing.

Charity, he writes, 'demands justice: recognition and respect for the legitimate rights of individuals and peoples. It strives to build the earthly city according to law and justice. On the other hand, charity transcends justice and completes it in the logic of giving and forgiving' (*CV* 6).

Just as, when we love someone, we desire that person's good – their welfare and their fulfilment – and take concrete steps to secure it, in the same way a requirement of justice and charity is to desire the common good, that is, the good of society as a whole, and to take concrete steps to bring it about.

'To love is to give,' says Pope Benedict, 'to offer what is "mine" to the other ... I cannot give what is mine to the other, without first giving him what belongs to him in justice ... Justice is the primary way of charity' (*CV* 6). The way to achieve this, the Pope goes on, is to practise a form of politics.

> The more we strive to secure a common good corresponding to the real needs of our neighbours, the more effectively we love them. Every Christian is called to practise this charity, in a manner corresponding to his vocation and according to the degree of influence he exerts in the *polis*. This is the institutional path – we might also call it the political path – of charity, no less excellent and effective than the kind of charity which encounters the neighbour directly, outside the institutional mediation of the polis. When animated by charity, commitment to the common good has greater worth than a merely secular and political stand would have. Like all commitment to justice, it has a place within the divine charity that paves the way for eternity through temporal action. (*CV* 7)

The particular *kind* of politics to which Pope Benedict calls all Catholics is not an optional matter, because it flows from the Christian witness to love of neighbour. It's not about seeking political office (worthy though that is), or voting (necessary though that is), but primarily about building the power of civil society to imbue the state and the economy with the values and virtues of justice. Democracy and the market are not machines that run by themselves; and when they are left to themselves, operating in a vacuum of legitimacy, unaccountable, they tend to run amok, detaching themselves from the values and purpose for which they exist. A healthy democracy and a human economy require active, organised citizens, people imbued with habits of heart and mind, and equipped with the arts and skills of public action, to hold them to account.

That's the 'political path' which the Pope is describing. It's something bigger than party or electoral politics – 'a merely secular and political stand' – because it is 'animated by charity', by a form of love.

Love. It's a not a word often associated with politics. Yet those who attend the assemblies of London Citizens are struck by this 'extra' quality, something transcendental, which they might call a glimpse of 'the world as it should be', or which Catholics might describe as 'a vision of the City of God'.

It's the sight of ordinary people gathered for a common human purpose, a concern for the poor and vulnerable in the city. It's the way that people of different faiths and none are able to unite around common concerns, or the way pragmatism and ideals combine in campaigns and actions that are small but concrete steps towards the world-as-it-should-be.

This 'extra' quality attracts people to London Citizens, and explains why people give their time to it. Love in action is why dozens of Catholic parishes, charities and schools every year renew their membership of London Citizens, and attend training courses; and why parishioners and schoolchildren with their priests and bishops take part in 'actions', meetings, trainings and assemblies.

A simpler way of putting it – and Catholics in London Citizens put it this way all the time – is that London Citizens is 'Catholic social teaching in action'.

Catholic social teaching is dynamite: a coherent set of principles, inspired by faith, accessible to reason, but rooted in human and political reality and valid for all people. Solidarity, subsidiarity, intrinsic human dignity, participation, the option for the poor – these are the values of human coexistence, the cement of society.

Once you put this stuff at the heart of your thinking, it explodes all the '-isms' of the modern world. Here is wisdom rooted in tradition and capable, for that reason, of being truly radical. Pope Benedict XVI describes CST as *caritas in veritate in re sociali* – 'the proclamation of truth of Christ's love in society'. The love of Christ, notoriously, was not reserved to a particular group of people or faith, but spoke and speaks to the root of what is human.

The Church has always had a social teaching. Just hear Basil of Caesarea in the fourth century thunder against the subprime lenders of his day, the rich landowners who stored up grain in a time of scarcity to drive up prices, then lent money to peasants at usurious rates so they could buy it. Usury, says Basil, 'involves the greatest inhumanity, that the one in need ... seeks a loan for the relief of his life ... While searching around for antidotes, he came upon poisons. It was your duty to relieve the destitution of the man, but you increased his need.'² That's social teaching.

But what we know as CST is more specific. By common consent, it dates back to 1891, when Pope Leo XIII decided to speak out on the growing gap between rich and poor which had resulted from the Industrial Revolution. His great encyclical, *Rerum Novarum*, was promulgated at the time Cardinal Manning was intervening in the East End of London to broker the Great Dock Strike, and giving speeches about the just wage. It was a time like our own, when the world shrank through technological advance (the steam engine and the ship propeller at that time; the microchip in ours), massive immigration and emigration, and a free-market dogmatism, justified by social Darwinism, which believed that what was good for the market was good for everyone – especially when it came to wages. Cardinal Manning stood with the Church in all times against that 'anthropological error', arguing that basic human need, not the market, should determine a just wage.

Manning's witness and writings impressed Leo XIII, and was one of the formative influences on *Rerum Novarum*. That first, foundational encyclical identified the anthropological errors which underlie injustice, and laid out vital principles which are the lodestars of a moral, just, civilised coexistence. Every Catholic should know them.

But the tragedy is, they don't. That's why *Faithful Citizens* is as much about exploring the key principles of CST as it is about showing how London Citizens advances those principles in both its aims and its means. It is about the *values and vision* of CST made real through the *method* of community organising in contemporary London.

Community organising? It's an odd term. It became a little less odd during Barack Obama's 2008 presidential election campaign, when it emerged that as a young man he had learned his remarkable political skills working as a community organiser in the South Side of Chicago. His Republican opponent, the Governor of Alaska, Sarah Palin, poured scorn: 'What's a community organiser?' she mockingly asked. And immediately badges appeared on Democrats' lapels saying, 'Jesus Christ was a community organiser; Pilate was a governor'. What was little mentioned – by Democrats as well as Republicans – was that Obama had worked for a coalition of Catholic churches, and had his organiser's salary paid for by Cardinal Bernardin, then Archbishop of Chicago.

There are around 65 'citizens' organisations' in US cities, built by community organisers, which are major players across the US, bringing about a better deal for the poor on housing, jobs, immigrants' rights, wages, and so on. And Catholic congregations and organisations play a major role in them.

Community organising has proved, in the United States, to be the primary means by which Catholic parishes, schools and charities have been able to expand their influence over the decisions which affect them and their communities, and to move the world further in the direction of the vision and thinking of CST. And their bishops back them with funds and vocal support.[3]

These citizens' organisations are not charities dispensing services to the poor, but alliances of those same charities and congregations, which enable ordinary people with passion and drive to learn and practise the art of politics through real negotiations with mayors and local authorities and businesses. They have learned how to build power, and how to use that power to help bring about the principles of CST.

In the US, these 'peoples' organisations' are called 'faith-based community organisations' (FCBOs). In the UK, and increasingly in the US, they are also known as BBOs – 'broad-based organisations'. It doesn't really matter what we call them, as long as we grasp what they are. They have names such as East Brooklyn Congregations (EBC) in New York, or Baltimoreans United in Leadership Development (BUILD) in Baltimore. Each has anywhere between 60 and 300 organisations, mostly faith congregations, in membership. They are led by the people who run these organisations: priests and pastors, nuns and lay people, directors of charities, or just ordinary people in parishes. Like London Citizens, they are affiliated to the Chicago-based Industrial Areas Foundation (IAF), which trains the full-time organisers hired by the BBOs to train ordinary people in the arts of public action.

Organisers and leaders. These are the two key roles in a BBO. A *leader* is a director of a charity, or a parish priest, or a religious sister, or a chaplain, or an ordinary parishioner with vision. Most people don't think of themselves as leaders, but that's one of the tasks of the organisers – to find people like you, and encourage you to think of yourself as a leader. The *organisers* are the technicians of a BBO. They are employed because they are good relationship-builders. They are skilled at helping people see themselves as leaders, training and encouraging them to act as public people.

The brilliance of community organising – the reason it is so effective – is that it organises around *people*, not *issues*. That's why it fits so well with CST.

Think about most political or social action and you'll realise that it's the opposite. Saving whales, deforestation, war protests, campaigns on climate change, human rights – it's almost always the issue that comes first. People cluster around a cause because they care about the issue. But then the issue goes away, or the cause fails, and everyone disperses; and the group is no more powerful than it was when it started. The only thing that bound them together was the shared concern about that issue.

Community organising starts the other way round. It first brings people into relationship with one another, around shared values and concerns; then it deepens that relationship through common action on an issue which is important, at that time, to that set of people. When the issue disappears, the relationships are still there, and stronger – and the BBO is ready to tackle another issue. Each time, it grows in strength and makes new relationships. It becomes more powerful. As it does so, civil society is strengthened, becoming more organised. And the vicious cycle of social fragmentation, powerlessness and injustice begins to be reversed.

We'll leave the history of community organising to Chapter 2. For now, it's enough to point out that Catholic churches have played a strong role in broad-based organising ever since the pioneer of community organisations, Saul Alinsky (1909–72), first brought together Catholic parishes and labour unions in the South Side of Chicago, with the backing of the local bishop. Over the decades, and especially since the 1970s, community organising has grown and grown – not just across the US, but now to London, Berlin and Sydney. In Berlin, a Catholic priest is the lead organiser of the Deutches Institut für Community Organizing (DICO), which has sponsored two alliances of congregations and charities in that city.[4] In Sydney, the Catholic archdiocese of Sydney under Cardinal Pell has contributed large funds to the establishment of the nascent Sydney Alliance.

Older than either of these is CitizensUK,[5] a training institute for BBOs in Britain, of which the largest and most permanent is London Citizens. London Citizens was created 14 years ago in East London by a sponsoring committee set up by, among others, Bishop Victor Guazzelli, then the Catholic auxiliary of East London, and Bernadette Farrell, known to Catholics for her liturgical music. Prominent Anglicans and Muslims also played their part in the 1996 creation of TELCO, as it was first called. London Citizens nowadays includes not just the original East London alliance, but also South London Citizens (established 2004) and West London Citizens (2005).[6] North London Citizens is currently in formation.

Bishop Guazzelli was concerned about the state of his patch in the East End of London – Tower Hamlets and Hackney. He tried to organise his priests and people to effect change. But Catholics were a small minority, and the achievements were limited. Then he got wind of an initiative in south-west England, where Neil Jameson, who had learned community organising at the Industrial Areas Foundation (IAF) institute in the US, had created the 'Communities Organised for Greater Bristol'. Bernadette Farrell, who was advisor to Bishop Guazzelli, went to see Neil. 'A shiver went down my spine,' she recalls. 'This was it. This was what we had been looking for.' A committee was formed to raise money, and Neil was recruited to begin community organising in East London.

Basil Cardinal Hume, then the Archbishop of Westminster, backed his auxiliary bishop's initiative, and was at the launch of TELCO in November 1996. He paid tribute to its vision, which included, he said, the recognition of a common humanity, the need to act together, and the belief in the possibility of change. On the second point he stressed the task of restoring and building civic relationships – strengthening civil society. In CST, it is only when civil society is strong that the market and the state will know their place, and when justice can come. And that strength rests, above all, on strong relationships of trust.

Cardinal Hume was clear about what was needed.

> In our society today there are many forces pushing people apart. We live at a time of social fragmentation and division, where more and more people live alone, family stability is threatened, and employment is insecure. Adversity and difficulties can easily drive people apart, and place relationships within families, and within and between communities, under stress. The possibility of mutual trust, and therefore of mutual commitment, is undermined. This is a profound impoverishment of what it means to be human, for we all need friendship, and often we must act together if we are to achieve social change. What may be impossible for an individual, or even one local community group to do alone, may in fact become achievable if enough people come together with common aims.[7]

This is what community organisers mean by 'power'. Power is the ability to act. In French and Spanish, *pouvoir* and *poder* are verbs meaning 'to be able', as well as being nouns meaning 'power'. A broad-based organisation (BBO) such as London Citizens is about building power – the capacity to act together to solve common problems.

The reason people feel (and are) powerless is because they lack that ability to act together. And the reason they lack that power is because the bonds uniting them are feeble. As Pope Benedict says, 'As society becomes ever more globalised, it makes us neighbours but does not make us brothers and sisters' (*CV* 19). Relationships in the modern city are fragmented. That's not our fault. We're under pressure. We battle with multiple demands on our time. Bad transport and job insecurity, professional success, exhaustion – sound familiar? 'Coming together with common aims' scores pretty low in our list of priorities.

Yet we do this when we attend Mass, when we give time to our local community, when we attend meetings. A person that never joins others with common aims is a lonely person indeed. If it is important to us, and if we see that it works, most of us would be happy to join with others occasionally to make something happen that makes the world a better place. But most of us don't know where to begin, and are understandably suspicious that doing so will ever produce results.

That's why BBOs have professional organisers – to do the time-consuming work of bringing people together, discovering what matters to them, and enabling them to act on it. The genius of community organising is that it doesn't demand of people what they're not capable of giving, while activating their skills and gifts so that the limited time they can give is spent fruitfully. As well as being a vehicle for social change, a BBO is a teaching organisation – nurturing leaders, giving them the equipment and experience they need to build relationships that bring about change.

Since Cardinal Hume helped to launch TELCO, London Citizens has steadily grown stronger, to include (at the time of writing) just over 150 member organisations – parishes, schools, mosques, charities, trade union branches etc. – in its city-wide alliance. It has trained more than 2,000 leaders in the art of politics and negotiation using tested methods derived from decades of experience from the US.[8] And it has become a major player in the politics of the capital, persuading mayors and banks and local authorities to make changes urged by the member organisations.

Among the Christian denominations, the enthusiasm of the Catholic response to London Citizens has been striking. The reason is CST. It's not just because CST believes strongly in justice, and gospel values – the same is true of Anglicans and Methodists and Salvation Army members (and there are plenty of these parishes and charities in London Citizens). It's because CST offers a vision for a local politics of the common good in which people of different faiths and none work together for change.

This is a vital point. CST is a set of values for all humanity, inspired by and enlightened by faith, that act as the cement of society. It is not an easy idea to grasp: this is a *Catholic* teaching which is intended for, and appeals to, *all people*, whatever their faith or lack of it. CST identifies the common values which enable people to live together – people of all faiths and none – in peace and justice. Those values are a means of embracing all men and women as they are, in respect and love, and offer a means of acting politically on that truth. CST principles go to the root of the human being as he and she lives in society.

Because Catholics have CST as part of their cultural background, they respond readily to a vehicle – London Citizens – which embodies those principles and puts them into action. At the same time, those principles allow people of all faiths and none to work together. 'Catholic social teaching has been one of the great strengths of London Citizens,' says Mgr John Armitage, a parish priest in the East End of London and TELCO pioneer. 'It's about organising people together to work for the common good, inspired by Catholic social teaching. Those principles are the common language we speak, and because they speak to human experience they are able to unite trade unions, mosques, synagogues, and schools – all different values-based institutions which seek to build the community. Catholic social teaching provides the truth, the insight, that enables us to act together, working together for the good of all.'

Catholics are not as familiar with CST as they should be. And the reason for this ignorance, ironically, is that CST fell into disfavour in the 1960s precisely because it was seen as sectarian and confessional.

Let's go back. The heyday of CST was in the 1920s–40s, when it offered a 'third way', an alternative set of principles and insights to the prevailing ideologies of the day – liberal individualism, or the collectivism of Left and Right. You may recall the names: Catholic Action, Young Christian Workers (YCW), the Catholic Worker movement – among others – were all attempts to live out CST, and left a profound legacy. Some are still going. But both they and CST fell off the radar of modern mainstream European Catholicism in the 1950s–60s.

Before the Second Vatican Council in the 1960s, CST operated on a confessional, institutional model. That wasn't the fault of CST, but of the Church's defensive position in European society, and an historic attachment to state privileges. Catholic Action was a kind of lay arm of the bishops; its members were exclusively Catholics, and while it strove for the common good, it sought to do so primarily by trying to influence the state. The mentality was part of the 'fortress Catholicism' of the day.

Ironically, CST – which is a set of universal, not confessional, principles – was placed at the service of confessional and institutional interests.

There was a good reason for this. The rise of the totalitarian state, of both Left and Right, prevented a politics of the common good. The Church needed a vehicle to defend its freedoms, and battled with communism and fascism by creating alternatives – Catholic trade unions, Catholic political parties (before they were squashed by authoritarian states) and Catholic associations of every kind were attempts to safeguard and promote a space for the Church within a society which the state sought to shape in its own (pagan) image. In this battle it wasn't what united you with others, but what made you different, that was important.

After the Second World War, that battle was largely over. The triumph of democracy meant the Church regained its freedom. A politics of the common good was finally possible.

But CST was tainted by its association with a non-democratic era. The activists of social Catholicism entered the state, or political parties such as the Christian Democrats. In the 1960s, the Second Vatican Council definitively overturned the model of fortress Catholicism, embracing church–state separation and religious pluralism. Now Catholics were called to work with others of goodwill for the common good. But they didn't have the habit, and decades of fortress Catholicism meant they lacked the vehicle. They had the fuel and the roadmap, but didn't have the car.

It was different in the United States.

In America, unlike Europe, Catholics were long used to cooperating with other faiths. Church–state separation, and the fact that they were in a minority, meant that Catholics were not tempted by a politics aimed at winning the state. The Catholic churches which got involved in community organising back then and since are used to working with Protestants and Muslims for the common good. They've been doing community organising for decades and have developed a wealth of techniques and experience which CitizensUK now teaches to organisers and leaders of London Citizens. Across the US, there are broad-based people's organisations in which Catholics have played a major – and often decisive – role. In short, they have the car.

Now there is a British version of that car in London, a vehicle for enabling us to work for social change on the principles of CST. It looks a bit different from its American cousins, as British vehicles do, but the same principles operate in both. A BBO such as London Citizens has no official faith: it acts as a vehicle for the values and interests of its members which are able to come together around the principles of CST. It works best precisely in the conditions of diversity and pluralism which now prevail in London.

That is also why community organising has come of age in Britain. London nowadays looks a lot like modern American cities: rapid economic growth, influx of immigrants, rising property prices, growing violence on the streets, a widening gap between rich and poor – and a society of ever greater diversity, in which a third of the city's population has been born abroad. Community organising works in London because it addresses the very issue that holds back social change – the lack of organisation which is the result of the dislocation of communities. A disorganised society is one in which the market and the state call the shots. To rebalance the power of money and the state, civil society must organise and hold both to account. But it can only do that by investing the time in building the relationships which have been dislocated. That's why London Citizens works.

CST, too, is poised for a 'second spring'. In the midst of a global economic crisis with strong social and political ramifications, it is undergoing something of a revival. The parallels between the Victorian age in which Leo XIII issued his great call and our own are too great to ignore: then, as now, rapid dislocation followed on the heels of economic growth, globalised capital and immigration. The very issues which *Rerum Novarum* and Pius XI's 1931 encyclical *Quadragesimo Anno* addressed are the ones which face us now.

The argument of this book is that the fuel and roadmap offered by CST have found a perfect vehicle in community organising.

It is time to bring the two together between covers.

In the US, there have been many academic studies of community organising and its effects on religious congregations,[9] just as there have been books written by Catholic community organisers.[10] But there is no practical guide linking community organising and CST which can be used in parish groups or by parish leaders, one which gives lay people citations from encyclicals and official church documents, then shows how these are put into practice in contemporary London.

Part I of this book gives an introduction to the principles underlying both CST and community organising. Meet the fuel, then the car.

Part II takes the car on the road, showing how London Citizens has brought about significant changes in applying these principles in its political actions. Each of the five chapters has a number of stories, which illustrate both the principles of community organising and those of Catholic social teaching. Each of these chapters ends with a focus on an important CST document.

Chapter 3 is about subsidiarity, the way in which civic friendship is deepened through the 'relational' politics practised by London Citizens. It begins with the story of how South London Citizens overturned a spiral of violence in south-east London, teaches some principles of the 'one-to-one' relational meeting which is at the heart of community organising, and shows how one-to-ones can transform parishes.

Chapter 4, 'Assembling in solidarity', concerns CST's call to participation and the obligation on ordinary Catholics to be active, responsible citizens. It homes in on one of the most distinctive features of community organising – the big public assembly – and shows how such assemblies enable exactly this. It explains the principles and objectives of the assembly, and shows how these were put into practice in a big assembly in the Barbican in November 2009.

Chapters 5, 6 and 7 each take an issue – wages, housing and immigration – and show how CST treats each of these, and then how London Citizens campaigns advance the cause of the dignity of the human person, which is at the heart of CST.

Chapter 5, 'The just wage is a living wage', is the story of the London Citizens living-wage campaign, for which the organisation is best known. The London Living Wage is based precisely on Pope Leo XIII's principle of a just wage, which starts from need. This chapter has many stories of living-wage 'actions' by London Citizens, illustrating some of the maxims of community organising – and the kind of fun that citizen politics can be.

Chapter 6, 'Dwelling in dignity', takes two London Citizens housing campaigns and tells more stories of actions and negotiations bringing CST alive. Both the 'Our Homes Our London' campaign for community land trusts and the 'Housing Our Future' campaign to reduce overcrowding in Wandsworth show more community organising principles in action on an issue of huge importance to contemporary London.

Chapter 7, 'Welcome, stranger', is about immigration, an issue of great contemporary importance and on which CST has much to say. We tell the story of two London Citizens campaigns – a citizens' enquiry into the Lunar House immigrant processing centre, which developed into a national campaign for a fair and humane asylum system; and the Strangers into Citizens campaign, born out of a Mass for Migrant Workers at Westminster Cathedral, which calls for a conditional amnesty for long-term undocumented migrants.

The Conclusion suggests ways in which *Faithful Citizens* can be used in parishes and schools and other Catholic communities. Appendices list the documents and principles of CST for easy reference, as well as some maxims of community organising. A bibliography and list of web links give some directions for the onward journey.

Like CST itself, *Faithful Citizens* is a call to action – to the great adventure of love and fellowship which is citizen politics. It is intended to blow off the lid, and release some of the dynamite contained in Catholic institutions when they unite with others, on the principles of and at the urging of CST, to love and serve the world that begins at the narthex.

Enjoy the ride.

PART I

1 CATHOLIC SOCIAL TEACHING: A DEEPER KIND OF POLITICS

All members of the Catholic Church must accept their full share of responsibility for the welfare of society. We should regard the discharge of those responsibilities as no less important than fulfilling our religious duties and indeed as part of them.

Catholic bishops of England and Wales[1]

Fine, but how? You can vote, and carefully making up your mind before you do is one very necessary way of being a faithful citizen. You can meet your MP – which is good, if he or she will see you, but probably rather frustrating, because it's just you, or just your organisation, and yours is one of many voices. Then there's justice and peace work, and no shortage of brilliant Catholic and other organisations that need you to write letters, and join campaigns. But how do you 'do' the politics envisaged by Catholic social teaching (CST)?

If CST remains outside the mainstream of ordinary parish life, seldom referred to in the pulpit, almost never mentioned in the RCIA pro-gramme for people becoming Catholics, and very unlikely ever to be taught as part of catechesis and formation programmes, it is partly because the principles seem abstract. They are universal principles, aimed at western, post-industrial society in general. They are not just guides to a politics of the common good, but also to the means of bringing about that good. Yet in the absence of a vehicle for translating them into action, CST risks being something only referred to every six years in bishops' docu-ments issued prior to elections – guides to voting, in other words, but of little impact on the lives of ordinary Catholics in between.

Most Catholics are barely aware that the Church offers a 'set of princi-ples for reflection, criteria for judgement, and directives for action' (*Sol-licitudo Rei Socialis* 41) on the major social, political and economic questions of the day. Few could tell you that wages should not be left to the market alone, or that popes throughout the twentieth century deplored a widening gap between rich and poor. They might not realise that the successors to St Peter believe in the access of all to private property, and they might be very surprised to hear that they condemn the lending of money at exorbitant interest rates.

For those that stumble upon CST, the shock can be immense, akin to stubbing your toe on buried treasure. CST is a sustained attempt to understand how societies function and the principles that should guide them. It is the fruit of tradition, of the early church writers through to modern theologians, of the many Christians struggling to live out their faith in justice in a world often marked by alienation, commodification, and exploitation.

CST is once again coming to the fore of Catholic consciousness, in part because of the banking crisis which hobbled the world economy in Autumn 2008, in so many ways analogous to the economic crisis of the 1930s which followed on from the stock market crash of 1929. In this case, it is not senseless stock market speculation but reckless lending, a detaching of money from people, that has brought the financial system to its knees. Now, as then, the sober discovery is that we had trusted in idols: the market, left to itself, would somehow generate prosperity for all. Pius XI wrote the second great social encyclical, *Quadragesimo Anno* (*QA*) in 1931, but he might have been referring to the liberal utilitarian dogmatists of 2009 who believed that an unregulated market, freed from its fetters, would over time deliver benefits for all.

> Just as the unity of human society cannot be built upon class conflict, so the proper ordering of economic affairs cannot be left to the free play of rugged competition. From this source as from a polluted spring have proceeded all the errors of the 'individualistic' school. This school, forgetful or ignorant of the social and moral aspect of economic activities, regarded these as completely free and immune from any intervention by public authority, for they would have in the market place and in unregulated competition a principle of self-direction more suitable for guiding them than any created intellect which might intervene. (*QA* 88)

The call, then as now, is for the restoration of what *Quadragesimo Anno* calls the 'guiding principle of economic life', the 'true directive principle of social and economic activity', which is the human person. CST can be considered one long essay on that principle, a polemic against the myths and idols of unbridled market capitalism, or the spurious political utopias which it has provoked in response: communism, fascism, and so on.

It is an argument against subordinating human well-being to economic principles, whether of Left or Right.

But it has to be *applied*. CST itself is like a pair of glasses; look through them, and issues come into focus. The purpose of CST is to present the transcendental moral horizon people need to keep in view. It doesn't offer technical solutions, but guiding principles. There are many ways of translating those principles into action on issues – and the contention of this book is that community organising is one of the best.

What CST doesn't call for is endless discussion in seminars. 'The social message of the Gospel must not be considered a theory, but above all else a basis and a motivation for action,' writes John Paul II in *Centesimus Annus*. 'Today more than ever, the Church is aware that her social message will gain credibility more immediately from the witness of actions than as a result of its internal logic and consistency' (*CA* 57).

Without a vigorous civil society and active citizenship, however, the *application* of CST is problematic. It's like having high-octane fuel and a road map, but no car to take you there. Community organising is the car; it's a vehicle for social transformation.

But before we get the car out, let's take a closer look at the fuel.

What is CST?

Modern CST dates back to 1891. This does not mean that before 1891 popes ignored social topics. But *Rerum Novarum* inspired a broader and deeper commitment by church members to the dislocation and inequalities produced by industrialisation. Its impact was so great as to mark off the era which followed it from the one that preceded it. It marked the beginning of the Church's *modern* social teaching.[2]

As church teaching, its purpose 'is to contribute to the formation of conscience as a basis for specific action'.[3] It is expressed not in the language of revealed religion but of natural law, meaning that the truths it expresses are accessible to anyone, not just those who share Catholic religious presuppositions. Although they didn't say so explicitly until Pope John XIII's 1963 *Pacem in Terris*, the encyclicals have been addressed to 'all people of good will'.

That's why it would be frustrating for the insights of CST to be dismissed as 'Catholic beliefs'. The truths of CST are not like, say, the doctrine of the resurrection or the Church's teaching on the Eucharist; they are not taught as true because they have been revealed to the Church by Jesus Christ, but are accessible to human reason purified by faith. That said, CST since *Gaudium et Spes* has come to rely less exclusively on natural law, and now incorporates much more theology and Scripture: modern CST is much more Christ-centred, and therefore person-centred. Where the early encyclicals employed natural law arguments 'in an explicit, direct, and fairly consistent manner', CST since the 1960s 'has been explicitly biblical and its claims are drawn more often from the doctrine of Christ'.[4]

The main task of CST is to form consciences in the principles needed for fruitful human coexistence. As Pope Benedict says in *Deus Caritas Est*:

> Building a just social and civil order, wherein each person receives what is his or her due, is an essential task which every generation must take up anew. As a political task, this cannot be the Church's immediate responsibility. Yet, since it is also a most important human responsibility, the Church is duty-bound to offer, through the purification of reason and through ethical formation, her own specific contribution towards understanding the requirements of justice and achieving them politically. (*DCE* 29)

The Church's job is partly the prophetic one of creating stumbling blocks. When Leo XIII in 1891 spoke of long hours and poor wages placing a burden on workers 'little better than slavery itself', he is pricking consciences, drawing attention, as did the prophets of old, to what should be self-evident to anyone with eyes to see, yet not at all obvious to those who are blinded by a dogmatic faith in the free market or whose hearts are closed to the suffering in factories and mines. Indignation at the exploitation of human beings may be expressed by the popes in terms of the violation of God-given dignity; but you do not need to believe that human dignity is God-derived to share their indignation. An atheist can agree that child labour is bad.

The other task of the Church is to educate the consciences that it awakens. As George Weigel puts it: 'It takes a certain kind of people, possessed of certain virtues, to run self-governing polities and free economies so that they do not self-destruct. The task of the moral-cultural sector is to form these habits of heart and mind in people, and the primary public task of the Church is to form that moral-cultural sector.'[5]

The 'social question'

CST's core concern is what the popes call the 'social question', which emerged in northern Europe, the US, and other areas affected by the dislocation brought about by modern capitalism – emigration, industrialisation, urbanisation – in the nineteenth and twentieth centuries.

There are two main dimensions to this 'question'. The first is the alienation of capital and labour arising from the Industrial Revolution, when people left the land to sell their labour in cities to a minority of wealthy people who owned the capital and the means of production. The growing division of society into the wealthy few and the poverty-stricken many is what sparked Leo XIII's encyclical, and a large part of CST addresses the causes of that growing gap, causes which stem from an erroneous view of people as merely factors of production.

The second is the shrinking of civil society and the growth in the power of the state and the market, a process which has resulted in the increasing breakdown of society and the weakening of the mediating institutions (such as churches) which make life meaningful and hold the state and the market to account.

Most of the themes in CST arise from these two forces of modern western history. In the economic sphere, the themes in CST are the dignity of work, just wages, the duty of the state to correct the market, poverty, human rights, human development, rights of immigrants, and so on. In the political sphere, CST is concerned with the strengthening of civil society, the need for the state not to overwhelm and absorb mediating institutions, and the obligation on Christian citizens to participate in politics. These are the themes which receive the attention of CST, while others – such as racism, nationalism, feminism, etc. – are fairly scantily covered, although almost all the modern movements of emancipation find an echo in CST's concern to protect and enhance the intrinsic dignity of every human person.[6]

The documents

There is no established 'canon' of CST. What I have called below the 'classic' encyclicals would be included in any collection, as would be the 'global' encyclicals. Which others are worthy of inclusion is essentially a matter of choice and focus; the selection is broad and varied.

The documents referred to in *Faithful Citizens* are listed at the back under the following four categories:

1   *The 'classic' encyclicals*. These are the six papal documents – five encyclicals and one apostolic letter – spread over 100 years, on the 'social question', beginning with Leo XIII's *Rerum Novarum* in 1891 and ending with John Paul II's *Centesimus Annus* in 1991. Because

Rerum Novarum was promulgated in 1891, the five subsequent commemorative documents were all issued in the first year of the decade – *Quadragesimo Anno* in 1931, *Mater et Magistra* in 1961, *Octogesima Adveniens* in 1971, *Laborem Exercens* in 1981 and *Centesimus Annus* in 1991 – with many of their titles ('fortieth year', 'eightieth year') making clear that they are *Rerum Novarum* anniversary documents.

The classic encyclicals are letters by the pope of the day which offer analyses, explanations, diagnoses and prescriptions, in response to the social crisis triggered by modern capitalism. The nature of that crisis has differed from generation to generation, and what the popes choose to highlight varies in each document. But anyone who reads the documents together will be struck by the notes of continuity, and the way they refer back to previous popes' teaching. And the themes remain largely the same: the split between capital and labour, the division of society into haves and have-nots, the accumulation of property in the hands of a few, the role of the state, the importance of civil society, and so on. Unlike the 'global' encyclicals, which are a response to globalisation, the classic encyclicals are concerned with the advanced capitalist societies of Europe and North America – that is, with 'modernity', as it is understood.

2   *The 'global' encyclicals.* Whereas the classic encyclicals are concerned with social issues present within states, the global encyclicals from the early 1960s are concerned with issues on an international scale: political relations between states, and the post-war world order, especially the attempt to build peace in an era of superpower conflict, as well as what might be regarded as socio-economic issues of international development, immigration, technology, global capital, poverty, agrarian reform, etc. The key document in this series is *Popolorum Progressio*, recently commemorated by Pope Benedict XVI's *Caritas in Veritate* which described *PP* as 'the *Rerum Novarum* of the present age' – the age being, of course, one of globalisation.

3   *Roman documents.* This category includes three kinds of authoritative church teaching:

(i) Papal encyclicals from the 1970s through to the 1990s which are not social encyclicals *per se*, because they are concerned firstly with mission and evangelisation, and the Church's relations with the world as a whole. But they are usually included and referred to in collections of social teaching because they shed important light on that teaching.

(ii) Documents which have arisen from the deliberations of bishops from across the world assembled in Rome, the most important of which is a key document of the Second Vatican Council, *Gaudium et Spes*, which was concerned with the Church's relations with the modern world. Also significant is *Justitia in mundo*, a declaration of the Synod of Bishops meeting in Rome in 1971.

(iii) Significant documents issued by the various Vatican departments concerned with social issues, such as the Pontifical Council for Justice and Peace or the Pontifical Council for the Pastoral Care of Migrants and Itinerant People. These 'pontifical councils' were created in the 1970s to assist the Church's pastoral care of humanity. The key documents are summarised in the Council's *Compendium of the Social Doctrine of the Church*. Some of the fundamentals of the teaching are also summarised in the *Catechism of the Catholic Church*.

4   *Regional church documents*. This last category refers to the authoritative teaching of the local Churches, in the form of bishops' conference documents which apply Catholic social teaching to the social and political challenges of the present moment. In the UK and the US, it is normal for bishops' conferences to issue guidelines to voters at least six months before a general or presidential election; these are normally summaries of Catholic social principles and draw attention to particular issues. But there are also occasional teaching documents issued by bishops' conferences on specific issues, or in response to particular perceived social challenges. Listed at the back are some of the bishops' documents referred to in *Faithful Citizens*.

CST: changes over time

The main change occurred after the Second Vatican Council, when social teaching became concerned with international issues. Another key development since the 1960s has been the linking of preaching the Gospel to justice, such that Catholic social teaching itself is seen as an 'essential' part of the Church's missionary activity, and a form of evangelisation.

Perhaps the most significant shift – one that is striking when you read the texts – is the shift from a natural law language to one that is much more biblical. CST before *Gaudium et Spes* was expressed in exclusively philosophical and natural law terms, rather than biblical or theological language; since the 1960s it has remained in that tradition, but bases its claims on more explicit references to Jesus Christ. Pope John Paul II, for example, used Scripture more extensively in his encyclicals than any of his predecessors. In *Laborem Exercens*, he argues for the dignity of the person and human work from the insights of Genesis; in *Centesimus Annus*, he asserts the shared responsibility for all humanity in the Gospels of Matthew and Luke.[7]

Why this shift takes place has everything to do with the Second Vatican Council: a new openness to the modern world, a new attentiveness to historical context and development, a return to Scripture and a special emphasis on the dignity of the human person in the context of the new 'communion' theology of the time. From the 1960s, CST develops a new language which we might call one of Christian humanism: it becomes warmer, more dialogical, but at the same time more theological – and in many ways less accessible than the clear, ringing prose of Leo XIII and Pius XII.

A third shift in CST has been what might be called 'the primacy of love'. If reason was the primary shaper of the pre-1960s documents, love – *caritas* – has emerged as the heart of justice and the motivation to act on behalf of justice, and is the word that appears in the titles of Pope Benedict XVI's two social encyclicals, *Deus Caritas Est* and *Caritas in Veritate*. CST has come to rely less on the appeal of reason and truth – although clear reasoning remains a strength of CST – and more on the option of love which the heart makes for God. Reason is not discarded in CST, any more than is natural law. But both are put in their proper place: CST now starts from the overwhelming truth that, as Benedict XVI titled his first encyclical, 'God is love'.

A fourth shift has been evident especially in the pontificates of John Paul II and Benedict XVI, who have been concerned to heal the scandalous division of modern Catholics – especially in the US and Europe – into two opposing camps, one 'pro-life', the other 'pro-justice'. *Caritas in Veritate* makes clear that it is a contradiction to care about one unless you care about the other (*CV* 28). This is a recovery of what Cardinal Bernardin of Chicago called the 'seamless garment' approach to life ethics, from 'womb to tomb'. How we treat unborn human life, the elderly, undocumented migrants, those living under the yoke of unjust wages or usurious interest rates, those excluded from public life by virtue of their race or disability – this is all essentially CST, for it is concerned with the upholding of the dignity of human life in the face of the forces seeking to degrade it by turning it into a commodity.

Finally, CST has moved over time towards emphasising praxis, or action. It is not enough to have the correct view of a situation (orthodoxy) – by studying and reading, for example. Reflection needs to lead to right action (orthopraxis), which is then evaluated and reflected upon, and leads to further action. The pre-1960s' methodogy of CST ran the risk of 'social idealism', isolating reason from a relationship of dialogue with experience, commitment and action. In the postconciliar – since the Second Vatican Council – view of CST, the starting point of reflection needs to be people in their struggle, in their needs and in their hopes, and moving as swiftly as possible to concrete action.

A sketch

It's hard to reduce CST to ten key principles, but I've attempted to do so in Appendix I. They're there to refer to any time during this book when you want to explore them further – or be reminded of what makes CST dynamite. For now, we'll point to the main documents and what they were about.

The foundational document of CST, *Rerum Novarum*, recognised that there were three key factors in economic life – labour, capital and the state – and that the justice of the relationship between the three is the crucial issue in a politics of the common good. Justice was served neither by a liberal ideology which believed in leaving wages to the market alone, nor by a socialist ideology which sought to hand over property to the state. The right order was one in which private property was spread through just wages, and which allowed workers to organise to increase their bargaining power with capital. Leo XIII believed that the state should intervene to correct the market; he had less to say about the importance of organising civil society – though he praised trade unions.

In his 1931 encyclical *Quadragesimo Anno*, issued in the midst of the rise of European dictatorships, Pope Pius XI commemorated *Rerum Novarum* by confronting the issue of social inequality and calling for the reconstruction of the social order along the lines originally set out by Leo XIII. CST at the time was sometimes spoken of as occupying a 'third way' between free-market capitalism on the one hand and the statist ideologies of communism and fascism on the other. There is truth in that description: certainly, Catholic Action and the social Catholic movements of the day were conscious of carving out an alternative to the prevailing clash of ideologies – between liberal individualism and the collectivism of Left and Right. But *Quadragesimo Anno* calls for the repair of relations between labour and capital on the basis of justice and cooperation, primarily through a reinvigorated civil society, and a state which intervenes for the sake of the common good to assist, but not absorb, civil society institutions – a principle known as subsidiarity.

After *Quadragesimo Anno* is another long gap of 30 years. Pope Pius XII published no social encyclicals but contributed to CST through a series of radio broadcasts during and after the Second World War in which he outlined a just world order necessary for global peace and the moral basis for democracy. Both the United Nations and the European Economic Community were born of this era, and Pius XII strongly supported the collaboration which these new organisations promoted. His focus was on establishing the post-war democratic, pluralistic order.

Pope John XIII wrote two major social encyclicals which address three challenges of the 1960s: economic recovery, decolonisation, and the Cold War. *Mater et Magistra*, commemorating *Rerum Novarum* on the eve of the Second Vatican Council, set forth principles to guide Christians and policy makers in addressing the gap between rich and poor nations and threats to world peace. John XXIII portrayed rights not just as legal and political but also social and economic – the right to work and a just wage, to participate, and so on. And he called on Christians to work with others to create local, national and global institutions which would respect human dignity and promote justice and peace. *Mater et Magistra* was followed, in 1963, by *Pacem in Terris*, which was concerned not just with peace but with 'new methods of relationships in human society'.

John XXIII's social documents mark a shift: until the 1960s Catholics in Europe tended to operate in exclusive associations or movements. In the US, because of the pluralistic nature of society and the tradition of community organising, Catholics were much more used to entering alliances with other Christians, and with other faiths and none, to secure their objectives. John XXIII was in effect endorsing and promoting that American model – the one which operates in community organising.

In 1962, John XXIII summoned representatives of the world's bishops to Rome for a major Council which was concerned with the pastoral question of how the Church could best serve humanity. During the years of the Council, the bishops became aware of the problems besetting the Church in all parts of the world. The social question was no longer firstly about capital and labour in the West, but also about the distribution of land in the developing world. For the first time in the Church's history, this was the gathering of a genuinely world Church, and CST would thereafter take on a stronger global dimension. As the Second Vatican Council document *Gaudium et Spes* memorably begins:

> The joys and the hopes, the griefs and the anxieties of the men of this age, especially those who are poor or in any way afflicted, these are the joys and hopes, the griefs and anxieties of the followers of Christ. Indeed, nothing genuinely human fails to raise an echo in their hearts.(*GS* 1)

The delegates saw a world polarised by ideologies and threatened by nuclear war. They saw the effect of the Cold War, spiralling arms costs, environmental degradation, and the growing disparity between rich and poor. And they recognised that the Church, by virtue of its mission, had a unique responsibility for shaping the values and institutions in the world order.

In retrospect, it's possible to see that the bishops were meeting at the end of the Enlightenment – all those '-*isms*' had played themselves out in European history, culminating in the totalitarian horrors of the twentieth century, the graveyard of the ideologies. The Church in this time had turned inward, often confined to the private sphere where it had been relegated by secular society. During the Second Vatican Council, the bishops rejected that role, affirming that the mission of the Church gave it 'a function, a light, and an energy which can serve to structure and consolidate the human community according to the divine law' (*GS* 42). But it did not seek to proclaim this truth, as it were, in a vacuum, but to undertake a new collaboration with other faiths and people of goodwill, in a new context of religious pluralism and freedom.

Paul VI's *Populorum Progressio* in 1967 was the foundational document of that postconciliar, global social teaching. It responded to the cries of the world's poor and addressed the structural injustices which lay behind the social divisions. *Populorum Progressio* promoted the idea of 'integral human development', appealing to rich and poor nations to work together to establish an order of justice, and created a new Vatican department, the Pontifical Council for Justice and Peace, to encourage it.

Paul VI's *Octogesima Adveniens* was written on the eightieth anniversary of *Rerum Novarum*. It acknowledged the difficulties of establishing a new social order and emphasised the responsibilities of local Christian communities, working in partnership with all people and organisations of goodwill, to work for change. Reflecting on the nature of post-industrial society – urbanisation, emigration, unemployment, discrimination, and so on – Paul VI called for a greater share in decision-making, for action to hold politicians to account. *Octogesima Adveniens* asked Catholics to evaluate what was going on in their society, reflect on it in the light of the Gospel, and to work, in collaboration with others, to change it. It called on Catholics to become political: 'Politics are a demanding matter – but not the only one – of living the Christian commitment to the service of others,' wrote Paul VI. 'Without of course solving every problem, it endeavours to apply solutions to the relationships men have with each other.'

This call to Catholics to 'go public' was another significant historical shift. Throughout the nineteenth century and much of the twentieth century, the Church had faced hostile states and been relegated to the margins of public life. The public square was not a place Catholics wanted to be, or were often allowed to be. The Church had adopted a siege mentality, a fortress attitude, which Paul VI was now calling on them to abandon. In the new post-war democratic climate, his message was that Catholics needed to work with others of goodwill: to proclaim the Gospel was at the same time to declare a vision of humanity and a new social order. In the same year as *Octogesima Anno*, the bishops gathered at a Synod in Rome declared that 'action on behalf of justice and a participation in the transformation of the world fully appear to us as a constitutive dimension of the preaching of the Gospel' (*JM 2*).

This idea of a Church that acts to promote justice as an integral element of its faith is strongly present in the regional and international gatherings of bishops, especially of the Latin Americans gathered at Puebla (1968) and Medellín (1979). It was as a result of these Conferences that the preferential option for the poor – an idea first mooted in *Popolorum Progressio* although always implicit since *Rerum Novarum* – passed into CST. It meant not just that the poor have a special claim on the Church's attention, but that the poor challenge the Church to conversion, service and solidarity. The option for the poor requires changes in unjust political, social and economic structures, as well as personal conversion.

'If the hours of labour have no other object but the gain of the employer,' Cardinal Manning once wrote, 'no working man can live a life worthy of a dignified human being.' John Paul II's first social encyclical, *Laborem Exercens*, was a powerful reminder of Leo XIII's original ringing defence of the human being as not merely a factor in production. He asserted 'the priority of labour over capital' and criticised an 'economism' that sought to reduce human beings to mere commodities. The encyclical was a strong critique both of liberal capitalism and of collectivist socialism, and an essay on the dignity and value of work.

In *Sollicitudo Rei Socialis*, John Paul II commemorated the twentieth anniversary of *Popolorum Progressio*, contrasting progress and development, and arguing against a materialist conception of economic growth. His 100-year *Rerum Novarum* anniversary encyclical, *Centesimus Annus*, was published in 1991, after the collapse of socialism in most of Eastern Europe but not yet in the Soviet Union. *Centesimus Annus* explored and expanded the concept of solidarity – or the principle of 'civic friendship' – as a key theme in CST.

The encyclical is a close analysis of the failures of communism, arguing that violation of workers' rights, the inefficiency of state-controlled production and the spiritual void of atheism had all contributed to the collapse of socialism. But he warned against replacing it with consumerist capitalism, signalling the alienation which arises from social relationships marked by competition, estrangement, and the using of people as means to an end. Capitalism, he pointed out, has multiple meanings. If capitalism means recognising a positive role for business, the market, private property endowed with a sense of responsibility and free human creativity, then it is positive; but not if it means an economic system which is free from the constraints of a strong juridical framework which directs it in the service of the common good. And he warned – prophetically in the light of the financial collapse of 2008 – against the return to blind faith in markets:

> The Marxist solution has failed, but the realities of marginalisation and exploitation remain in the world, especially the Third World, as does the reality of human alienation, especially in the more advanced countries. Against these phenomena the Church strongly raises her voice … The collapse of the communist system in so many countries certainly removes an obstacle to facing these problems in an appropriate and realistic way, but it is not enough to bring about their solution. Indeed, there is a risk that a radical capitalistic ideology could spread which refuses even to consider these problems, in the a priori belief that any attempt to solve them is doomed to failure, and which blindly entrusts their solution to the free development of market forces. (*CA* 42)

Under Pope Benedict XVI, there have been two important social teaching documents: *Deus Caritas Est*, which is concerned with the Church's charitable outreach to humanity, and *Caritas in Veritate*, an anniversary encyclical commemorating the fortieth anniversary of *Populorum Progressio*.

Caritas in Veritate has been published in the midst of a major economic and financial crisis, with its roots in what Pope Benedict sees as a tragic loss of trust and solidarity in the global market. Just as *Rerum Novarum* criticised individualism and blind faith in markets, *Caritas in Veritate* deplores the way in which the market has been detached from its human purpose; and, like *Rerum Novarum* and all the social encyclicals since, calls for a restoration of a true humanism:

> Only a humanism open to the Absolute can guide us in the promotion of and building of all forms of social and civic life – structures, institutions, culture and *ethos* – without exposing us to the risk of becoming ensnared by the fashions of the moment. Awareness of God's undying love sustains us in our laborious and stimulating work for justice and the development of peoples, amid successes and failures, in the ceaseless pursuit of a just ordering of human affairs. God's love calls us to move beyond the limited and the ephemeral; it gives us the courage to continue seeking and working for the benefit of all, even if this cannot be achieved immediately and if what we are able to achieve, alongside political authorities and those working in the field of economics, is always less than we might wish. God gives us the strength to fight and to suffer for love of the common good, because he is our All, our greatest hope. (*CV* 78)

Caritas in Veritate is in many ways a radical document. It identifies justice through redistribution as the heart of politics, an essential complement to wealth creation. Politics must intervene to ensure that business serves the common good. The Pope calls, as did his predecessors, especially John Paul II, for a vigorous civil society practising the virtue of solidarity. 'The exclusive binary of market-plus-state is corrosive of society,' Pope Benedict observes, 'while economic forms based on solidarity, which find their natural home in civil society without being restricted to it, build up society' (*CV* 29). The principle which liberates the potential of civil society is subsidiarity – what we might call the 'free-association' principle, or 'principle of civil society'. Subsidiarity, he says, is the antidote to both an overweening state and market hegemony. It is for the Church in its social teaching, Pope Benedict says, 'to reawaken the spiritual energy without which justice, which always demands sacrifice, cannot prevail and prosper' (*CV* 56).

After more than a century of CST, the Church is now placing its emphasis on the formation of a civic political culture. 'Catholic democratic theory has, in the main, focused on structural questions of participation, representation, voting rights, the rights of association, and so forth,' said George Weigel in 2004. 'With these questions largely resolved, the focus must now be on the priority of culture: on the institutions of civil society and their capacity to form genuine democrats.'

All of which seems like a good opportunity to get the car out.

2 AN INTRODUCTION TO COMMUNITY ORGANISING

> We learn, when we respect the dignity of the people, that they cannot be denied the elementary right to participate fully in the solutions to their own problems. Self-respect arises only out of people who play an active role in solving their own crises and who are not helpless, passive, puppet-like recipients of private or public services.
>
> Saul Alinsky[1]

Community organising is a method by which ordinary people engage with politics through their institutions – churches, neighbourhood associations, unions – which form an alliance in order to promote the common good. Community organising is the means by which those institutions in turn form people as democratic citizens. The citizens' organisations which it builds are the vehicle by which they, through their institutions, transform society.

President Obama, who worked as a community organiser for an alliance of Catholic and other churches in a poor area of Chicago, gave a speech many years later in which he deftly summarised what community organising does and achieves.

> Organising begins with the premise that (1) the problems facing inner-city communities do not result from a lack of effective solutions, but from a lack of power to implement these solutions; (2) that the only way for communities to build long-term power is by organising people and money around a common vision; and (3) that a viable organisation can only be achieved if a broadly based indigenous leadership – and not one or two charismatic leaders – can knit together the diverse interests of their local institutions.
>
> This means bringing together churches, block clubs, parent groups and any other institutions in a given community to pay dues, hire organizers, conduct research, develop leadership, hold rallies and education campaigns, and begin drawing up plans on a whole range

of issues – jobs, education, crime, etc. Once such a vehicle is formed, it holds the power to make politicians, agencies and corporations more responsive to community needs. Equally important, it enables people to break their crippling isolation from each other, to reshape their mutual values and expectations and rediscover the possibilities of acting collaboratively – the prerequisites of any successful self-help initiative.

By using this approach, the Developing Communities Project and other organizations in Chicago's inner city have achieved some impressive results. Schools have been made more accountable; job training programs have been established; housing has been renovated and built; city services have been provided; parks have been refurbished; and crime and drug problems have been curtailed. Additionally, plain folk have been able to access the levers of power, and a sophisticated pool of local civic leadership has been developed.[2]

London Citizens is another such vehicle. The UK capital's largest alliance of faith congregations and civic institutions is affiliated to the Chicago-based Industrial Areas Foundation (IAF), which was founded as a training institute for professional community organisers by Saul Alinsky, who pioneered the methods the IAF still teaches today. In the 1970s the training programme for organisers and leaders became rooted more deeply in faith institutions and their values, and organisers concentrated on building stable, long-lasting community organisations. The fruit of this work is a network of 'broad-based organisations', or 'faith-based community organisations' as they are known in the US, which includes dozens of institutions, mainly church and other faith congregations.[3] There are now around 65 FBCOs/BBOs – among them London Citizens – affiliated to the IAF, seeking change in a large range of areas such as education, wages, housing, immigrant rights and health care. The growth of these 'peoples' organisations' has been particularly marked in recent years: most are less than 20 years old.[4]

Community organising is a method and set of democratic practices which enable people to resist the pressures of market and state, and defend their goods, by realising their own power, based on mutual relationships of trust. It has a particular approach to politics which is particularly suitable to act as a vehicle for CST, because it is deliberately unideological, emphasising action over theory, and because it *does* politics rather than just *talks* about it.

> *Political demoralisation occurs when atomisation prevails, when*
> *people find themselves outside institutions and organisations. It is*
> *only through the realisation of the importance of relationships, and*
> *the mobilisation of those relationships as forms of political power*
> *that people can change their urban environment and participate*
> *effectively in civic life. Only organised citizens can effectively resist*
> *organised crime. The most important corporate starting-point for*
> *that engagement are not political parties, which tend to dissolve*
> *into the state, nor pressure groups which become campaigning*
> *organisations, nor trade unions which often become national and*
> *remote. Neither is it the individual acting alone. The starting point*
> *are the local faith community congregations within a particular*
> *locality and their capacity to work together to re-moralise their civic*
> *environment.*[5]

A key concept in the training given by IAF/London Citizens concerns the tension between 'the world as it is' and 'the world as it should be'. To be political is to be able to live in both worlds simultaneously, and endure the tension between them. It means being clear-eyed and realistic about the world, which operates according to power and self-interest rather than love and altruism. (It doesn't take refuge, as so many ideologies do, and as religion can do, in an idealised or abstract view of the world and human beings.) And it means keeping at the same time an eye on the ideals and values which are written on the human heart and described in Scripture as the Kingdom of God. Leo XIII captures this 'politicalness' in *Rerum Novarum* with his maxim: 'There is nothing more useful than to look at the world as it really is – and at the same time look elsewhere for a remedy to its troubles' (*RN* 14).

This is the Christian understanding of politics. Christians in the early Church thought of themselves as 'resident aliens' in the world, honouring just rulers, obeying just laws, and contributing to the common good of their society, yet with an ultimate loyalty to a Kingdom that is elsewhere. St Augustine's medieval classic *City of God*, whose citizens have one foot in the earthly city and the other in the heavenly city, was the vision for politics in the medieval era. The Christian citizen needs to operate in both spheres simultaneously.[6]

Community organising draws on this same idea of politics, nourished by the values of faith congregations, and led by people who live in 'the world as it is' yet look to 'the world as it should be'. Valuing the vision of the 'world as it should be' contained in religion – while also honouring the ideals of secular visions – is one of the keys to its vitality and success.

Saul Alinsky

To understand how community organising came about, let's glance briefly at the man considered its pioneer and architect, a Chicago sociologist and criminologist called Saul Alinsky. According to Luke Bretherton, Alinsky's life's work – the creation of 'peoples' organisations' – betrayed four key influences.

The first was where he grew up. Alinsky was the child of Russian Jewish immigrants in Chicago whose culture was derived from the Shetl traditions of Eastern Europe.[7] Family was strong, as were local community institutions, which were committed to the welfare of their society. They took seriously the words of Jeremiah 29:4–7: 'Seek the welfare of the city where I have sent you into exile, and pray to the Lord on its behalf, for in its welfare you will find your welfare.' In Chicago at the time, the interests of the community were advanced through churches, synagogues and mutual associations.

The second, surprisingly, was organised crime. Alinsky was fascinated by it. As a sociologist at Chicago University, he spent time with teenage Italian gangs on the West Side of the city, learning how they worked. They were hard for police to break up because of the tight personal relationships and the trust that they spent so much time developing. In his work in the poor South Side of Chicago – site of the first broad-based organisation he created in 1939, the Back of the Yards Neighbourhood Council – Alinsky used these same techniques of relationship-building in organising the poor to resist the criminal gangs. Unlike the gangs, the organisations Alinsky created did not use violence to further their ends; but they weren't afraid to apply every other sort of pressure. These confrontation strategies are recounted in his writings, which are full of delightful stories of apparently powerless people turning the tables in their favour.[8]

Chicago at the time was highly 'disorganised', a city of rapid social change and dislocation following on waves of immigrants and capital, with parents on low wages working two jobs, rapacious landlords, feral children, violence and insecurity. Street gangs were natural in this context, as they are in many parts of London today, a city also marked by mass immigration, the power of capital, a bureaucratic state, political demoralisation and so on.[9] A key need of young – and not so young – people is for recognition and respect; without parents and other figures in authority to give it, it will be sought from peers and in delinquent behaviour. Only by organising itself could a community contain the criminality of gangs. That meant reconnecting young people to families and institutions, and organising the neighbourhoods so that they could work together in pursuit of common goods instead of against each other and against their own best interests. And it meant giving recognition to people, helping them see themselves as leaders capable of making change.

> *What Alinsky had spotted was that in poor communities, the strongest institutions with the deepest roots were faith-based; they provided vital resources to poor communities – a measure of dignity and a sense of meaning in lives scarred by poverty. Find a way to connect them and you have the power to bring about change.*[10]

Alinsky created the Back of the Yards Neighbourhood Council (BYNC) in 1939, with crucial support from an auxiliary Catholic bishop, Bishop J. Sheil, who persuaded local parish priests to back the project. Nine out of ten people in the area were Catholics, but they were strongly divided on ethnic and other lines. Union leaders, local churches and local businesses were brought together, and won many concessions from City Hall to improve local services.

The BYNC had a number of characteristics that are still true of broad-based organisations today. It was self-financing, independent of any political party or interest, and run by local leaders; it put time and resources into the training of local leaders drawn from local neighbourhood institutions, especially churches and clubs; it brought into alliance those institutions, especially those with strong values; and it organised actions and campaigns on issues directly affecting local residents – wages, crime, housing, and so on.

The third influence on Alinsky, according to Bretherton, was organised labour. From labour unions Alinsky also learned the importance of public assemblies, and of focusing attention on the issues which were of central concern to the people living in the area. Alinsky saw organising labour as a means of gaining real power for the disenfranchised, but it was his idea to link the labour movement with faith congregations.

If you google Alinsky, you will find not a few 'Catholic' websites which condemn him as a communist, and which delight in pointing out that he

dedicates his *Rules for Radicals* to Lucifer. He was certainly not a communist; he once went to meet the future Paul VI to give him ideas on how to
combat communism in the labour movement in Milan. But he *was* a
hell-raiser. He loved to shock and confront. His mission was to overturn
the tables, and puncture the respectability behind which the wealthy and
the powerful liked to hide. And he challenged religion to do the same. The
dedication of his book *Reveille for Radicals* is typically mischievous: 'Lest
we forget, at least an over-the-shoulder acknowledgement to the very first
radical,' he wrote, 'from all our legends, mythology and history ... the
first radical known to man who rebelled against the establishment and
did it so effectively he at least won his kingdom – Lucifer.'

It was intended to shock. Alinsky believed that before real change could
occur, people had to get over the idea that it was somehow wrong to rebel.
He wasn't praising Lucifer for rebelling against God; he was praising
Lucifer for having the courage to shake things up. Theologically, that's not
such a strange idea; God in the Old Testament after all 'sends' Satan to test
his people, such as Job. And the Son of God, when he comes on earth, does
a fair of bit of table-overturning himself. Alinsky's quote is designed to
jolt those who believe God is always on the side of a human status quo – a
theological temptation which particularly besets those Christians who
benefit from leaving things as they are. The irony of these 'Catholic'
websites condemning Alinsky as a satanic communist because of this
quote is, of course, lost on them.

Not only was Alinsky not a communist, but he was a passionate
advocate of democracy – the third major strand in his thinking. His
democratic vision could be taken straight from *Quadragesimo Anno*, in
which people articulate their interests and values not just as individuals
but as part of what *Quadragesimo Anno* calls 'intermediate institutions'.
Like the popes, he rejected the French Revolutionary conception of
democracy as the state on the one hand, and atomised
individuals on the other. Alinsky believed that democracy works well only
when people in institutions came together in alliances to agitate for
change:

> Democracy is that system of government and that economic and
> social organisation in which the worth of the individual human
> being and the multiple loyalties of that individual are most fully
> recognised and provided for. Democracy is that system of
> government in which we recognise that all normal individuals have
> a whole series of loyalties – loyalties to their churches, their labour

unions, their fraternal organisations, their social groups, their nationality groups, their political parties and many others.[11]

Alinsky deplored the fact that the Left had no account of the common good. The socialist vision of the interplay of capital and labour was that of inevitable class conflict, and, like the capitalists they fought against, reduced people's interests to the purely economic. In Alinsky's view, they failed to see democracy – an arena of peaceful interplay of interests – as the proper place in which to advance the lot of the ordinary person. In *Reveille for Radicals*, he wrote:

> Every conceivable effort must be made to rekindle the fire of democracy while a few embers yet glow in the gray ashes of the American dream. Once it goes out it may take generations before a new fire can be started. The fire, the energy, and the life of democracy is popular pressure. Democracy itself is a government constantly responding to continuous pressures of its people … When we talk of democratic citizenship we talk and think in terms of an informed, active, participating, interested people—an interested and participating people is popular pressure!

> A people can participate only if they have both the opportunity to formulate their program, which is their reason for participation, and a medium through which they can express and achieve their program. This can be done only through the building of real People's Organizations in which people band together, get to know one another, exchange points of view, and ultimately reach a common agreement which is the People's Program. This is the reason for participation: their reason—their lives and the lives of their children. The universal premise of any people's program is, 'We the people will work out our own destiny.'

> This is the cardinal basis of democracy, and various specific issues are not too important in comparison with the main issue. *Can there be a more fundamental, democratic program than a democratically minded and participating people?* Can man envisage a more sublime program on earth than the people having faith in their fellow men and themselves? A program of co-operation instead of competition?[12]

Alinsky's concern, in other words, was much broader than improving the lot of the poor. True, he had an 'option for the poor' long before the term was coined: it was the disenfranchised whom he organised, because it was they who – because they were excluded from the networks of productivity and exchange – were most affected by the power of capital, or the predatory actions of the criminal gangs and the corrupt politicians. But what he developed was a not a sectarian or communal politics, but what Bretherton calls 'a local politics of the common good', organising Polish Catholic parishes into alliance with Lithuanians, Slovaks and Irish associations and the communists in the local labour unions to pursue a living wage and just working conditions. Although himself an agnostic Jew, Alinsky sought to work within the experience and the values of the community he was organising, which he learned through many hours of careful listening to the priests and leaders of the neighbourhood.

That's how CST came to be the fourth strand in his thinking. As Bretherton points out, 'For Alinsky it was through the interaction between democracy and Christianity that he was able to realise and articulate his politics of the common good and his distinctive approach to organising.'[13] Most of his important backers were bishops (Bishop Sheil, auxiliary of Chicago at the time) and he had a great friend in the leading European Catholic thinker, Jacques Maritain. And it has been churches that have been at the forefront of the community organisations which Alinsky built in his lifetime and since.

CST has long stressed the importance of the parish as a 'mediating institution', connecting families to public life. Although he could be critical of the churches, in them Alinsky found the basis for common action: committed relationships beyond political and economic self-interest; strong values; loyalty; and a capacity for mobilisation. 'The only major institutions fighting for justice, decency and equality in America are the churches,' Alinsky wrote in 1966. 'The labour unions are no longer doing it … They have become part of the status quo.'

His friend Jacques Maritain in the 1930s–40s was the leading Catholic philosopher of his day, a neo-Thomist whose thinking laid the groundwork for European Christian democracy in post-war Europe.

They admired each other, and became close friends. Maritain was convinced that Alinsky's method offered 'a new way for real democracy, the only way in which man's thirst for social communion can develop and be satisfied, through freedom', and described his *Reveille for Radicals* as 'epoch-making'.[14] He praised Alinsky as 'a great soul, a man of profound moral purity and burning energy, whose work I consider the only really new and really important democratic initiative taken in the social field today'.[15]

Alinsky's neighbourhood councils embodied Maritain's vision of strong intermediate institutions acting to check the centralising and totalising thrust of the modern state; and they both trusted the wisdom and judgement of ordinary people over technocrats and ideologues – an embodiment of what Maritain called 'political fraternities' independent of the state.[16]

Alinsky could be abrasive and cynical, and his advocacy of tension and conflict – although always peacefully, and for good ends – was not part of CST, which is also intended for people living in states where peaceful protests can be life-threatening.[17] But Maritain saw Alinsky's methods as fundamentally compatible with CST: they were 'good and necessary means to achieve good and necessary ends'. He knew what drove Alinsky: 'the deep-rooted motive, power and inspiration of this so-called trouble-maker is pure and entire self-giving, and love for those poor images of God which are called human beings'.[18] Not only were Alinsky's community organising efforts heavily backed by the archdiocese of Chicago –- just as today BBOs receive major funding from the US bishops[19] – but Maritain introduced him to Archbishop Montini of Milan, later Pope Paul VI, with whom Alinsky spent a week in Milan 'discussing the Church's relationship with local communist unions'.

After his initial success in Chicago, Alinsky created the Industrial Areas Foundation (IAF) with support from Bishop Sheil and philanthropists. In the 1940s–50s, he created a number of organising projects in New York, Montana and California, which scored significant successes in stemming racial tensions and violence and in winning gains in wages for immigrant farm labourers. In 1960, a coalition of local Protestant ministers in Chicago asked Alinsky to set up a community organisation in Woodlawn, a large black community. The Woodlawn Organization made use of picketing and boycotts to confront local landlords and merchants, and organised to stop plans by the city and the university for local renewal in the area, forcing the city to give the group representation on a school board and an anti-poverty agency. The Woodlawn Organization won significant improvements in sanitation, public health, police practices, and its fame led to Alinsky being asked to train more community organis-ers and to start IAF projects.[20] Community organising began to spread across America, giving local people a much greater say in the decisions which affected their lives.

Alinsky died in 1972, leaving an inspiring legacy of organising, and two texts which are a blueprint for building democracy: *Reveille for Radicals*

(1946) and *Rules for Radicals* (1971). He had created community organisations as political institutions with three basic characteristics: indigenous leadership and citizen participation; financial independence; and a commitment to defending local interests while avoiding divisive issues. His genius was to take organising into poor communities and to play a no-holds-barred power politics based on confrontation as a means of gaining recognition and to forge compromises with power-holders. By confronting the state and capital, and winning concessions for ordinary people, he made democracy more real.

But there were weaknesses in Alinsky's model. The first was that, while churches made up the bulk of the membership of his organisations, he was not especially interested in the institutions themselves. The job of Alinsky's organisers was to forge coalitions of institutions, get the projects up and running, and then leave, passing on responsibility for organisational development to the institutional leaders. This meant that the IAF at Alinsky's death was weak, and many of the organisations he had created did not last.

A new model was called for, one that combined both interests *and* values, and which would lead to stable citizens' organisations. Ed Chambers, who took over the IAF, developed a new model, one that combined self-interest with religious beliefs, and which looked more explicitly to CST for the values and programme the IAF would promote.[21] At the same time, it became socially broader. Chambers recalls:

> In the 1980s, IAF started changing the size and scale of organising. We began to build broader and deeper organisations. We recognised moderates and the middle class as untapped potential. Organising only poor people couldn't produce enough power. Large citywide or countywide geographic areas were targeted. We hold on to Saul Alinsky's insight of building new organisations from the pockets of power that institutions already in the field represent. As a new generation of talented men and women organisers gained confidence and experience, they sought out and engaged all faiths, races, and classes. The poor, working class, middle class, and – to the horror of some ideologues – the wealthy and successful came on board.[22]

Chambers and another organiser, Ernie Cortes, both committed Catholics, decided to engage very directly with CST and the theological basis of organising, and root it more deeply in scriptural reflection. A series of retreats and seminars by another of the IAF's lead organisers, a Catholic priest, Fr Leo Penta, in east Brooklyn, was also important in this process.[23] 'The new IAF approach did not reject self-interest as one critical basis for political action. But the IAF began to see the possibilities for religion to provide a set of value commitments to combine with practical self-interest.'[24]

Chambers argued that organising should emerge from the intertwined values of family and faith. In his 1978 training manual, *Organising for Family and Congregation*, he highlighted the values of dignity and justice, and the essential values which religious institutions contribute to politics. And he argued that through IAF organisations, families and congregations could defend and promote their values in the public arena. 'With the citizen's organisation (the IAF affiliate) as a context and as an instrument, families and congregations can move with dignity and confidence into the arena of institutional power,' he wrote. 'Families and congregations can fight for their values. Families and congregations can win.'[25]

Modern organising is thus much more explicitly centred on the core preoccupations of CST, namely how to renew politics and society through mediating institutions actively engaged in the political process. Organising grew out of institutions – such as parishes – which nourish and sustain committed, faithful relationships; nurturing these relationships requires virtue and moral vision. 'However good its intentions, a politics without such piety is pitiless and impoverished,' notes Bretherton. 'Conversely, piety without any politics is pitiful as it has no means to challenge, protect and pursue the very relationships it loves and values most in the face of their erosion and co-option by the market and the state.'[26]

A broad-based organisation (BBO) is not a lobby group for the poor, or for religious interests; nor is it *primarily* a campaigning organisation. It is a power alliance within which different traditions and interests in the civic sector can act together to bring about change for the common good. It is a place where politics is learned and practised – through training, actions, assemblies, campaigns, negotiations, and so on. Its purpose is to make the state and the market more accountable to civil society.

In America, the focus of these efforts is primarily local – neighbourhood, city and state-wide. The expansion of BBOs in the US since the 1980s has been remarkable: the IAF has grown from about 20 to 60 affiliate BBOs in different cities across the US.[27] In his book *Going Public*, Michael Gecan, one of the IAF's present-day full-time community organisers, describes the organisations which organisers help to build:

Our groups are made up of nearly three thousand congregations and associations and tens of thousands of ministers, pastors, rabbis, women religious, and top lay and civic leaders … They spend untold hours mastering and using the full range of public arts and skills. They learn how to listen to others, to teach and train their members and followers, to think and reflect on the issues and pressures of the day, to confront those in power who obstruct or abuse them, and to build lasting relationships with allies who support or reinforce them. As leaders in large and effective citizens' organisations, they practise how to argue, act, negotiate and compromise.[28]

The BBOs are alliances of the 'mediating institutions' which CST emphasises as essential for a healthy democracy. They exist to promote and protect the basic mediating institutions – family and parish – by helping these to act publicly. Ernie Cortes writes:

While we agree with the documents of Catholic social thought that it is important to give religious meaning to institutions, we hope that the Church will do more than proclaim its values to its people. It must have a strategy to create for them a culture which is a way of engaging others and themselves. It needs to create and inform what Richard Neuhaus calls a 'public square'. Human beings in society need institutions in society in which they can engage each other, reflect upon their values and experience, teach their lessons to each other, and act in concrete, specific ways. It is only in this way that they gain deeper insights into religious meanings.'[29]

The last major development in modern organising has been in what is known as 'institution-building' or 'parish development'. Classic organising ideally assumes strong institutions, that is, congregations where there are strong relationships and a cadre of lay leaders under the guidance of a far-sighted parish priest. But institutions are much weaker now than 30 years ago. Relationships are more fragmented, and people have less time to give each other, let alone others outside. In the 1990s, the IAF began to offer the services of its organisers for 'parish development'. Mark Warren writes:

The parish development process represented an organising effort to articulate and unite the congregation around the institution's goals and purposes, strengthen church finances, and bring forth new lay leadership to expand church activities. To accomplish these goals,

IAF organisers used the network's relational organising technique of conversation leading to action. Parish development processes helped to identify new leaders, build a consensus, and forge collective leadership for the church.

The demand for parish development 'squared well with Catholic social teaching,' he goes on, for CST

> had long stressed the central role of the parish church as a mediating institution to connect families to public life. Church institutions were to play a critical role in protecting the family in the face of state and market forces. Moreover, such institutions linked private and public life. According to Catholic social teaching, people could only achieve their full dignity and humanity through relationship in community, relationships structured by Catholic institutions.[30]

Modern community organising, building on Alinsky's legacy, has developed explicitly in the direction indicated by CST. It retains four essential characteristics which, combined, make it unlike any other organisation. It is *institutional*, in the sense that it organises in and through member organisations, mostly religious congregations of a variety of denominations, but including schools, charities, trade union branches, ethnic associations, tenants' associations, etc. It is *broad-based*, in the sense that it builds organisations (such as London Citizens) which are made up of diverse faiths, races, economic backgrounds, reflecting the pluralism of modern urban society. It is *relational*, in the sense that it explicitly teaches leaders how to build long-term relationships as a basis for common action, in the process strengthening its members as mediating institutions between people and public life. Finally, it is *non-partisan but intensely political*, in that it does not endorse candidates, support political parties, or receive funding from the state or political bodies, but rather exists to build and exercise power on behalf of its member institutions.

Let's see how this all actually works.

PART II

PART II

3 CIVIL SOCIETY: STRONGER, TOGETHER

That's what the leadership was teaching me, day by day: that the self-interest I was supposed to be looking for extended well beyond the immediacy of issues; that beneath the small talk and sketchy biographies and received opinions people carried within them some central explanation of themselves. Stories full of terror and wonder, studded with events that still haunted or inspired them. Sacred stories.

Barack Obama[1]

Consider firstly how parishes and schools in South-East London over-turned a spiral of crime and violence following the murder of a Catholic teenager.

Jimmy Mizen was buried on 21 June 2008, the seventeenth young person to die a violent death in London in the past year.

On its way to the Our Lady of Lourdes parish, the funeral hearse paused at the bakery where, on 10 May, the 16-year-old had been stabbed to death by Jake Fahri, 19. Jimmy's mother, Margaret, surveyed the shop where her son had bled to death in his brother's arms. His sister Saman-tha, 21, who has Down's Syndrome, laid a bouquet at the makeshift shrine outside the Three Cooks Bakery erected by Jimmy's classmates from Thomas More school, a Catholic comprehensive in Eltham. It was deco-rated with blazers and school ties.

Outside the church where Jimmy had been an altar boy, and where Barry and Margaret Mizen are eucharistic ministers, school friends waited at the gates. His five elder brothers – Danny, Billy, Tommy, Bobby and Harry – carried the wicker coffin, while his younger brother George walked behind, carrying Jimmy's picture in a football kit.

Jimmy knew his killer. On that fateful day he had gone to the shop to buy sausage rolls with his brother Harry; Fahri, a boy with an uncontrol-lable temper and a string of convictions, demanded he get out of his way. He hit Jimmy, but the brothers fought back, pushing him out of the shop. Fahri smashed his way back in using a metal advertising display, and threw a glass oven dish which shattered upon hitting Jimmy in the face. A splinter entered his neck and severed vital blood vessels. With blood pouring from his neck Jimmy ran into a bakery cupboard to protect himself from further attack.

'Out of all the horrible things which go through my mind, that is the part that gives me nightmares,' Margaret Mizen later recalled. 'The thought of Jimmy being so scared that he had to hide in a cupboard.' When Jimmy's older brother Tommy arrived at the scene, he had to pull open the door hard because Jimmy was holding it shut. Jimmy fell into his big brother's arms before he was eased onto the bakery floor. He died shortly afterwards.

South London Citizens was already meeting to discuss street violence. 'In Lewisham, the biggest concern was safety – and the statistics bear this out,' says Bernadette Farrell, South London Citizens lead organiser. 'From the many one-to-one meetings I had done, there was a clear sense of danger. I realised that we had to do something – that this was the issue.'

Some months earlier she had held meetings with local leaders from member institutions of South London Citizens in Lewisham – faith congregations (including the Mizens' church, Our Lady of Lourdes in Lee), as well as schools and a medical centre. 'We had already been going down to the bus depots because of people's fears about what happened on the buses,' Bernadette recalls. 'The next meeting was scheduled at Our Lady's for June – just a month after Jimmy's murder. The Mizens weren't at that meeting, because they were away. We agreed a plan of action, which was to hold lots of one-to-ones over the summer, and scheduled another meeting for September.'

One-to-one meetings are the staple of organising. Without them, organising cannot take place. If you regard them as a waste of time, you can't be an organiser.

One-to-ones are meetings without an agenda, but with a definite purpose: to find out what makes people tick, what they care about, where they get their passion. People tell their stories, why they came to be who they are; they reveal their concerns and passions, their anger and their ideals. An organiser invests more than half of his or her week in doing them. What happens as a result – meetings, actions, campaigns – is the fruit. But one-to-ones are the roots. There is no community organising – and no campaigns and actions and successes and assemblies – without them.

We described CST as high-octane fuel, and community organising as the car. One-to-ones are the wheels that enable the car to move – and to keep it on the road.

The team which Bernadette Farrell brought together was the result of the one-to-ones she had done. The team spent the summer doing more one-to-ones – with shopkeepers, local leaders, bus drivers and police. Then it was time for the second meeting in September – to which Mr and Mrs Mizen came. 'It was the first time since Jimmy's death that I felt hope,' Barry later said. 'We were captured by that meeting', said his wife Margaret.

In London Citizens, meetings always begin with 'rounds'. Each person introduces themselves, then says what's on their mind. Everyone is 'recognised'.

With the Mizens present, along with about 30 others from local churches and schools, it was a powerful rounds that day. 'We shared our experience of safety in the local area,' recalls Bernadette. 'We discussed the problem areas and we set priorities – everybody in groups listed half a dozen priority areas they wanted to work on. We then voted on the top two. The top two were to work with shopkeepers locally, and to work with young people in the schools. We decided we would start with the shops.'

The decision was related to what had happened to Jimmy. A leader at Our Lady's spoke of the need of 'safe havens' – places where young people knew they could flee from trouble and be safe. Barry Mizen, who runs a shoe-repair shop, recalled his experience many years before in Sidcup when there were problems with graffiti and disorder. People hadn't bothered reporting it, so the police didn't act. Once the local shopkeepers took the decision to report, the police started to act and the graffiti disappeared.

'We put these two ideas together. We went out in teams and had one-to-ones with shopkeepers to listen to what the problems were,' recalls Bernadette. 'We had started that process over the summer, so we had some idea. But we began systematically to walk around on Saturdays among the local shops, and learned what had been going on in the weeks before Jimmy's attack. The shopkeepers were delighted that people were taking the trouble to talk to them. We heard about drug-dealing and break-ins – one shop had had ten break-ins, another three. We said, "Did you report it?" They said, "What's the point?" We said, "This is the point. If you don't report it, there aren't the statistics which enable the police to act." '

From these visits came the idea of a pledge which the shopkeepers would sign and put up in their window – to report any crime, however small. By October all the shops in Burnt Ash Hill, where the attack had taken place, had pledged 100 per cent reporting of crime. 'There was a great sense of solidarity,' remembers Bernadette Farrell. 'We were offered free fish and chips and people spoke about Jimmy, about doing this for him.' Immediately the crime figures started to rise and the police began to respond. The team held meetings with police, reporting the intelligence they had gathered. The shopkeepers quickly saw the results. Burnt Ash Hill must be now the safest street in South-East London.

'The second stage was to go back to the shopkeepers with young people,' Bernadette continues. 'They asked the shopkeepers, "Will you look after us if we need protection?" That led to the "CitySafe havens" idea.'

In April 2009, 30 shopkeepers on Burnt Ash Hill signed a charter to become CitySafe havens. The scheme was officially opened by the Mayor of Lewisham on 10 May 2009, the anniversary of Jimmy's birthday.

You notice the stickers as you walk along the last road he ever walked. There's one in the newsagents, another on the door of his local pharmacy and a third in the barbers. The bakery has one. The church has two.

Each bears the same legend: 'CitySafe Haven: Dedicated to Jimmy Mizen'.

Each offers the same thing – reassurance that this community is guarding its streets, looking out for one another. This is an organised community. Only an organised community can defeat crime.

'Early evidence suggests that the scheme has had an impact,' reports *The Times.* 'One boy, concerned about gang violence, dashed into a takeaway shop and waited until the danger has passed. Another girl took refuge in a bakery when she felt she was being followed. Shopkeepers reported both incidents.'[2]

'We feel like we're reclaiming the public space from a disruptive minority that dominated,' says Bernadette.

The work has been done by a team drawn from Our Lady's church, St Andrew's URC, New Testament Church of God in Lee High Road, St William of York and St Winifred's primary school. 'At each point,' remembers Bernadette, 'we had different people joining the team – teachers, youth workers, shopkeepers and bus drivers.'

The team had started with 12 but within a year had grown to 60. They went to the Mayor of Lewisham in February 2009, who was keen to support the scheme. He urged them next to do the same in Lewisham and Catford town centres. In September, the Mayor declared Lewisham Town Hall the first 'safe haven' civic centre.

The scheme has spread across London. In November 2009 the Mayor of London declared his headquarters, City Hall, to be the 200th safe haven. 'Every organisation that joins this scheme is truly helping to make London safer,' Boris Johnson gushed.

Margaret Mizen says she has been approached by many charities seeking endorsement for one initiative or another. But 'South London Citizens has actually done something', she says.

Civil society

The place where people come together voluntarily to act in and around shared interests and values is called 'civil society'. There can be shared interests and values in a business, of course, as there can be in the state. But the relationships of the market and the state are essentially those of contract – legal, financial and bureaucratic. There is nothing wrong with contracts: they are necessary protections. But because they are designed to protect people, they are necessarily limited, and focused on self-preservation. A society worth living in cannot depend on contractual relationships.

If the basis of political and economic society is the *contract*, the basis of civil society is the *covenant* – maintained, writes Jonathan Sacks, 'by an internalised sense of identity, kinship, loyalty, obligation, responsibility and reciprocity.'[3] Unlike legal and economic relationships, civil society relationships are *covenantal*, not *contractual*.

Civil society is the bedrock of democracy, the glue that holds society together. It is neither public (state) nor private (economic) but made up of what are often called 'voluntary organisations' – churches, schools, charities, fraternal organisations, residents' associations, ethnic groups, trade union branches, and so on. The dynamic behind these organisations is not profit; nor are they paid for by the taxpayer. Civil society is bound together by the power of association – the bonds formed by values and common interests.

What are these bonds? In *Caritas in Veritate*, Pope Benedict XVI describes civil-society relationships as based on gratuitousness, 'the logic of gift', which is both the source of unity in the human community and the element which humanises politics and the economy:

> Because it is a gift received by everyone, charity in truth is a force
> that builds community, it brings all people together without
> imposing barriers or limits. The human community that we build

by ourselves can never, purely by its own strength, be a fully fraternal community, nor can it overcome every division and become a purely universal community. The unity of the human race, a fraternal communion transcending every barrier, is called into being by the word of God-who-is-Love ... (T)he logic of gift does not exclude justice, not does it merely sit alongside it as a second element added from without ... (E)conomic, social and political development, if it is to be authentically human, needs to make room for the principle of gratuitousness as an expression of fraternity. (*CV* 34)

Because civil society is where values, ideals and traditions are lived out and learned, religion and education are central to it. That is why faith congregations and schools are the bedrock of civil society, and figure so strongly in London Citizens along with trade unions, ethnic associations and charitable organisations.

In strong civil-society institutions, relationships revolve around something other than buying and selling, or services: what transacts within them are not goods but reciprocity of trust, gift and beliefs. Consider a parish meeting – of faith-group leaders, say; or a catechetics class; or a parish council – and ask why people are there, and what binds them together, what brings them out of their homes and into this public space, and the answer will not be money, or a contractual obligation. People will speak of a common purpose, a shared commitment, a 'belonging', which, they might say, comes from their faith. These relationships are the most important source of sacred meanings in human life because within them people are made aware of their connections to each other and to their place and roots. It is in these relationships that we become *persons*, in the CST sense of that word, meaning not an isolated individual but one with others: not just consumers or voters, but people who work together in pursuit of a common vision, bound together, at their best, by ties of gratuitousness.

These relationships are the glue of civil society. The stronger they are, the stronger is civil society.

The state and the market should serve and support civil society. But so powerful have both become that the reverse is true. A major function of community organising is to build the power – the capacity to act – of the 'mediating institutions' that make up civil society, so it can better resist the power of the state and market, and hold them to account . That's not because community organising is opposed to the state and the market.

Both are necessary, and good in themselves. But without a strong civil society to shape them, they will destroy themselves. Community organising builds that strength.

The importance of civil society in CST

CST has consistently emphasised the importance of the vitality of this civil sector and the threats to it of an over-mighty state and an excessively powerful market. In 1991, looking back at a hundred years of papal teaching, Pope John Paul II noted:

> According to *Rerum Novarum* and the whole social doctrine of the Church, the social nature of man is not completely fulfilled in the State, but is realized in various intermediary groups, beginning with the family and including economic, social, political and cultural groups which stem from human nature itself and have their own autonomy, always with a view to the common good. (*CA* 13)

What has weakened democracy in modern European history, according to CST, has been the diminishment of civil society, as both the state and the market have grown in power and influence. Pope Leo XIII and Pius XI in the two first classic social encyclicals, *Rerum Novarum* and *Quadragesimo Anno*, observe this trend with concern, seeing in the weakening of what CST describes as 'intermediate' or 'mediating' institutions the erosion of a healthy society.

This process was accompanied by an ideology, born in the French Revolution, which conceives of democracy as an interaction between the state and atomised individuals, shorn of their loyalties to those mediating institutions, and depending greatly on coercion and obligation – in short, the triumph of 'contract' relationships over 'covenantal' ones. In the 1920s–30s, dictatorship and totalitarianism were able to take root precisely because of this erosion, when relationships of reciprocity and gratuity were replaced by those of obligation and coercion.

> It was inadequate forms of democracy which made it possible for Lenin, Mussolini and Hitler to cheat, lie and bully their ways to power … If democracy is to work it must … be supported by a truly civil society, that is, with protection for personal rights and liberties which exist independent of and antecedent to political society and

provide the only sound basis for the latter. This civil society is one
founded on respect for person and family, a morally responsible
citizenry knowing its rights and fulfilling its duties, built up through a
network of voluntary organisations, social, political and economic,
and based on respect for morally responsible freedom.[4]

The market has its place, but it must be kept in its place, lest relationships
become commodified. The state, too, has its place, but it must know its
place, lest relationships become bureaucratised.

The state can exert controls over the market, but too often the state is
the slave of money interests. As Pope Pius XI observed in 1931, in times
not unlike the present:

> The ultimate consequences of the individualist spirit in economic
> life are those which you yourselves, Venerable Brethren and Beloved
> Children, see and deplore: Free competition has destroyed itself;
> economic dictatorship has supplanted the free market; unbridled
> ambition for power has likewise succeeded greed for gain; all
> economic life has become tragically hard, inexorable, and cruel. To
> these are to be added the grave evils that have resulted from an
> intermingling and shameful confusion of the functions and duties
> of public authority with those of the economic sphere – such as,
> one of the worst, the virtual degradation of the majesty of the State,
> which although it ought to sit on high like a queen and supreme
> arbitress, free from all partiality and intent upon the one common
> good and justice, is become a slave, surrendered and delivered to the
> passions and greed of men. (QA 109)

CST calls for a 'society of work, enterprise and participation' which 'is not
directed against the market, but demands that the market be appropriately controlled by the *forces of society* and the state to assure that the basic
needs of the whole society are satisfied' (CA 35, my emphasis). A strong
civil sector is the basis of a healthy society and a healthy economy;
economic contracts and state bureaucracies cannot hold a society
together in peace, nor increase its solidarity. Only civil society can do this,
because it rests on the logic of gift rather than the logic of the market and
the state. Pope Benedict warns of what happens when state and market
triumph over civil society:

> When both the logic of the market and the logic of the State come
> to an agreement that each will continue to exercise a monopoly over
> its respective area of influence, in the long term much is lost:

solidarity in relations between citizens, participation an adherence, actions of gratuitousness, all of which stand in contrast with *giving in order to acquire* (the logic of exchange) and *giving through duty* (the logic of public obligation, imposed by State law) ... The exclusive binary model of market-plus-State is corrosive of society, while economic forms based on solidarity, which find their natural home in civil society without being restricted to it, build up society. The market of gratuitousness does not exist, and attitudes of gratuitousness cannot be established by law. Yet both the market and politics need individuals who are open to reciprocal gift. (*CV* 39)

Because civil society is constantly under threat from both state and market, 'the economic forms of solidarity' need to be just as constantly rebuilt and strengthened. This is true in times of economic growth as much as in times of recession. Where capital flows, businesses are created and fold; people are employed, fired, employed again elsewhere; areas stagnate, recover and expand. People respond to these trends by uprooting themselves and moving, following the direction of opportunity, or fleeing dead ends. In an age of globalised capital, the forces disaggregating society, whether in times of growth or recession, are very powerful indeed.

In 1931, two years after the Wall Street Crash which precipitated the Great Depression, Pius XI looked back at the heady growth of the previous two decades, culminating in collapse and stagnation, and regretted how,

on account of the evil of 'individualism', as we called it, things have come to such a pass that the highly developed social life, which once flourished in a variety of prosperous and interdependent institutions, has been damaged and all but ruined, leaving virtually only individuals and the State, with little harm to the latter. But the State, deprived of a supporting social structure, and now encumbered with all the burdens once borne by disbanded associations, is in consequence overwhelmed and submerged by endless affairs and responsibilities. (*QA* 78)

Pius XI called for the 'reconstruction of the social order', emphasising the need to rebuild mediating institutions, and warning the state – this was the high noon of fascism in Europe – against absorbing and usurping the functions of mediating institutions, something he described as an 'injustice' and a 'grave evil'.

Paul VI, too, emphasised the effects of social disintegration, the new loneliness created by rapid urbanisation, the way that people increasingly divided into haves and have-nots, ignorant of each other; and how, in this atomised, fragmented world, social injustices and violence breed.

> Man is experiencing a new loneliness; it is not in the face of a hostile nature which it has taken him centuries to subdue, but in an anonymous crowd which surrounds him and in which he feels a stranger ... In this disordered growth, new proletariats are born. They install themselves in the heart of cities sometimes abandoned by the rich; they dwell on the outskirts, which become a belt of misery besieging in a still-silent protest with luxury which blatantly cries out from centres of consumption and waste. Instead of favouring fraternal encounter and mutual aid, the city fosters discrimination and also indifference. It lends itself to new forms of exploitation and of domination whereby some people in speculating on the needs of others derive inadmissible profits. Behind the facades, much misery is hidden, unsuspected even by the closest neighbours; other forms of misery spread where human dignity founders: delinquency, criminality, abuse of drugs, eroticism.
> (*OA* 10)

Pope Benedict sees in the current crisis the collapse of solidarity and mutual trust which are essential to the proper functioning of the economy: 'Without internal forms of solidarity and mutual trust, the market cannot completely fulfil its proper economic function. And today it is this trust which has ceased to exist, and the loss of trust is a grave loss' (*CV* 35). In calling for the market also to adopt relationships of trust and gratuity, Pope Benedict opens up a new theme in CST – that businesses can become more like civil-society institutions. The term he uses for this is the 'economy of communion'. An economy of communion is a more human-oriented market which depends more greatly on trust. Without trust, as the financial crisis has exposed, the market destroys itself.

The trust business

In modern Britain, the decline in the power and influence of civil society is one of the most pressing issues of our time, one that endlessly reappears at the top of people's lists of concerns.

Fear of violence on the streets is the most obvious sign of this. 'What happens when there's a breakdown of relationship is that no one thinks they should help,' says Matthew Bolton, lead organiser of TELCO. 'Trust and relationships are what makes a place safe.'[5]

A Joseph Rowntree Foundation survey in 2008 showed this up. Time and again people identified a lack of public spiritedness and social responsibility, the way 'neighbours no longer knew or looked out for one another' and people were left 'lonely and fearful'.[6]

One of the central tasks of modern community organising is the building of relationships within and between institutions. To do this, religious congregations need to join up, to pursue goods in common and promote shared interests. Only by investing time and energy in this relationship-building can trust and solidarity be rebuilt. The organising must first be around people, rather than issues. The task has to begin in the parish itself. It is not enough to rely on common values, or a shared faith. Until we *know* each other, hearing each other's stories, we are not organised enough to act together in the way they did in Lee.

Recently, a new parish council of about 25 people in a central London Catholic parish was appointed. Some had worked together on particular tasks, but most of the faces were new. The parish priest asked if I would organise some one-to-one training, and encourage them to do one-to-ones.

Many were suspicious, and only a handful turned up to the first one-to-one training. But for those that did, it was a revelation. I ran through the key points with them. This is an exercise in hearing each other's stories, and finding out what we each care about, I said. It was about listening, and sharing, and probing to find out why people did what they did.

I brought two people out in front of the others and asked them to begin. I froze them occasionally, asking the others to comment: *how is it going?* I asked them to look out for signs that people were not being 'personal' enough – sticking to safe subjects, or being very cerebral. They soon got into the stride, moving swiftly from 'what' questions (what do you for a living, how long have you lived in the area?) to 'why' questions (why did you volunteer for the parish council? Why did you give up your well-paid job to look after children? Why are you part of the St Vincent de Paul group?). People started revealing the 'sacred' core of themselves – their passions, and values, and anger.

One woman said she worked as an information officer in a public authority. Asked why she took that job, she answered that she felt it was important for people to have access to the right information. But why *you*? I asked. Why is that important to *you*? She hesitated, paused, and then said, with a hint of anger: 'Because I was adopted as a child, and no one ever told me. When I found out, I wanted to know who my real parents were, and where they were. I went and found all that information for myself.' And how did that make you feel? I asked. 'It was like coming into a clear light,' she answered. 'It changed my whole view of myself.'

She had chosen a career that matched her passion – to liberate people through the giving of proper information. The one-to-one had uncovered what was important to her. But it also showed she had deep empathy with anyone who was denied that information. She was a 'liberator', one who liked to emancipate others. And that is a great quality for a leader.

Those who came to that first training agreed to do three one-to-ones with the other parish councillors. I arranged a second training, this time for the sceptics. They were still sceptical, but now they were also curious, because the others had been so enthusiastic. I did the same training again, and their scepticism soon vanished. Soon, they, too, were doing one-to-ones. The effect on the parish council was dramatic. From being a group of people assembled for a task, they became a community of leaders able and willing to act together on shared passions and concerns.

Barry and Margaret Mizen have also turned out to be great leaders. They only came to that September meeting because they knew and trusted Bernadette. Their passion was clear: to ensure that Jimmy's death was not the end of the story. Through the Lee CitySafe campaign, they could turn the sorrow over a young life cut brutally short into concrete steps to ensure it didn't happen to other people's teenagers. But that campaign could never have happened if the relationships of trust did not first exist, relationships patiently built up by Bernadette and the leaders of the CitySafe team.

Those relationships have since been turned to other, broader issues, ones not limited to Burnt Ash Hill. The South London Citizens team in Lewisham has built a strong relationship with its mayor and the whole Council. They have encouraged the Council to adopt the London Living Wage for their employees, and to pass a motion in favour of the Strangers into Citizens campaign. They have become a political player in Lewisham. And what has happened in Lewisham has been repeated in other boroughs across London.

You don't need to go to Chicago to find out what this is about. Try much closer to home, Whitechapel. Here London Citizens uses exactly the same training and principles as Obama did when he worked as a community organiser. The ideas originated in 30s depression Chicago, when Saul Alinsky hit on a way to organise the most impoverished and marginalised communities to win power to improve their lives ...

His concept of organising can be boiled down quite simply: its aim is to move the world from how it is to how it should be. Its methods are entirely pragmatic: look for where people gather (churches, unions?), identify where those institutions have mutual self-interest and build on it for local achievable campaigns. Develop relationships – nothing can substitute for the face-to-face encounter. Listen. The paid community organiser (like Obama) is a talent scout for natural leaders and teaches the political tools.

If this sounds a little abstract, Matthew Bolton, a 25-year-old organiser at London Citizens, helps make it very concrete. From a state school in south-east London, followed by Cambridge, he ended up working with cleaners campaigning for a living wage. He describes his job as firstly finding unlikely heroes – such as the Jamaican great-grandmother who had seen four private cleaning companies come and go and knew more about her job than any of them. Secondly, linking them with unlikely allies – such as the local mosques attended by Somali cleaners. Then organising protests and demos; the result was the cleaners won themselves a 40% pay increase and sick pay for the first time.

What Alinsky had spotted was that in poor communities, the strongest institutions with the deepest roots were faith-based; they provided vital resources to poor communities – a measure of dignity and a sense of meaning in lives scarred by poverty. Find a way to connect them and you have the power to bring about change[7]

In recent decades, there has been increasing demand for the skills used by community organisers to be taught in parishes – how to conduct one-to-one meetings, house meetings, and common actions. Many of these are obvious: keep the focus on action; start and end on time; have an agenda. But some, like keeping the timekeeper separate from the chair, are not.

The discipline of the rounds, for example, would be alien to most meetings, parishes included. In most meetings, meetings begin without any recognition of those present, and no opportunity to hear, however briefly, what is on their minds. The message, however subconsciously, is that the business is more important than they are. Most people in most meetings don't know who most other people are; or if they do, they don't *know* them. The atomisation of wider society has been mirrored in the way we conduct our business. Reversing that requires focus and concentration – and training in relational methods.

What unites the practices and skills taught by London Citizens is that they enable people to develop the habit of relating publicly to each other, and build the relationships of trust – the 'social capital' praised by Pope Benedict XVI (*CV* 32). The most important of these skills is the one-to-one. Because contemporary society does not allow people time to listen to others' stories, their hopes and fears – at least not outside a narrow circle of friends and family – we have lost the habit that would have been natural to previous generations. A one-to-one seems strange, and counter-cultural; and until it becomes part of the culture of an organisation, it'll seem artificial and forced. That's why it has to be learned, practised and carried out systematically.

And what happens when you do?

Hear what Fr Sean Connolly did in his parish in the East End of London, and what happened to his parish. After that, there is an excerpt from an organiser's manual about the one-to-one which explains what it is, and what it isn't. Last, we have an American organiser's story of how one-to-ones reversed the fortunes of an ailing Catholic church.

The London parish priest's one-to-one story – Fr Sean Connolly, Diocese of Brentwood

When I arrived in the Catholic parish of St Margaret's, Canning Town as a newly ordained deacon in 1991, my parish priest gave me, among many other things, two responsibilities. I should preach each week. And two or three afternoons a week I was to visit people in their homes. It was to be a long time before I found the indispensable link between the two tasks.

When I returned to St Margaret's as parish priest ten years later, I was moving from a parish where I had six children preparing for First Communion to one that had more than a hundred. I was replacing two priests and a deacon. The responsibility was overwhelming. Looking back on the first two years, I realised I had turned into a manager: I spent a lot of time in my office chewing my way through the ever-growing paperwork, and responding to the daily crises. The only time I spoke to people close up was to ask them to do something. I had fallen into the classic trap of the task-orientated life. The administration of the parish was necessary; but a nagging feeling grew within that told me that if I didn't have time for people, then something fundamental was missing. It led me to perhaps the most important decision of my ministry: I needed to get out and meet people.

Back in 1991 I would consult the book that contained lists of parishioners and where they lived, then walk to the far end of the parish and begin knocking on doors. Most people weren't in. Those that were often stared at me blankly. Even for those who recognised me and welcomed me in, it was a great surprise. These days you don't often find a priest at your front door.

As a seminarian I had learnt the value of visiting from evangelical Christians. I could see that it paid dividends. Yet too often the purpose of those visits was a narrow one – the salvation of the individual. There was an agenda to the encounter, one which turned it into a task to be accomplished, and dehumanised the individual concerned.

The one-to-one relational meetings pioneered by community organisers, which I learned from London Citizens, could not be more different.

I selected people to visit more or less at random. They were people who, usually in minor ways, had come to my attention through something they had said or done. Sometimes it was simply people who had come to me to ask for something; having been given a glimpse of perhaps an interesting story, I would turn the tables and arrange to come and see them. I would often then ask them to suggest someone else I might visit. Quickly the network would grow. In more recent times I have taken to carrying a notebook and pen with me, especially at the weekend Masses, so that I can respond to what people say and do by taking their details and so having a constant supply of people to visit.

I would give the parish secretary a list of names, addresses and telephone numbers I had collected, together with a list of times and dates when I was available; her task was to match them up. This was not so easy but it had two key advantages. When the time came to go out to visit, whatever reasons I might have to squeeze that time (sometimes valid, other times not), I had to go.

Anyone who sets up a one-to-one has to deal with a quizzical look: why have you come to see me? The first response of many to a request from the priest to visit is a vague feeling of guilt: 'What have I done?' Once reassured, their next worry is: 'What would you like me to do?'

Another obstacle is the desire to turn the visit into a social occasion, preparing food and ensuring the rest of the family is present. So I usually have to make clear the nature and length of the visit, and the fact that I then have to move on and make other visits; there will be another time for a social gathering.

One-to-one meetings are not easy. With the best will in the world they do not happen naturally, but require detailed planning. People lead busy lives, especially in poorer areas where they juggle long hours at work, home life with several small children, and often some study so that they can better themselves. But when they happen, these one-to-ones are transformational like nothing else; which is why making space for them is so vital. So much of our lives is focused on what we do and are valued by how much we achieve. The one-to-one meeting is just for itself, even if other things do grow from it. In our technological age it seems absurdly labour-intensive and time-consuming. By its very counter-cultural nature, it is precisely what we should be doing in our churches.

There is much that has been written by community organisers about the thinking behind the one-to-one as the key tool for organizing institutions in order to increase their capacity to influence the world around them. But Catholics can read it in a slightly different way, through a sacramental theology of a communion of hearts and minds. What distinguishes CST from so many philosophies and ideologies of our day is its understanding of the human being as a person, that is, not just as an individual, but as one in relationship with others. 'God did not create man for life in isolation, but for the formation of social unity,' the bishops write (GS 32); yet so many forces in today's society – whether of the state or market – serve to isolate and alienate people from each other. The one-to-one repairs the torn fabric of society.

A one-to-one is a short (40–45 minutes) conversation between two people, which opens up their stories and their passions. When you come away you have a greater sense of what gets the other out of bed in the morning, what makes them tick, what is most important to them.

I learned a lot about these meetings from one of the first one-to-ones I had in the parish. I went to see a man I knew by sight but had never spoken to properly. He told me that he worked helping the elderly who had been in hospital to adjust to being at home again. In previous months we had been trying to get a campaign going that would focus on the care of the elderly in the community. I had written about it in the newsletter, spoken several times about it at Mass, and held a number of meetings to focus the campaign. This regular committed parishioner knew nothing of these efforts. Having taken the time to visit and speak with him I knew the future would be different. To me he would no longer be just another parishioner whom I vaguely recognised and whose name I might just remember; to him I was not just another priest who he only ever saw or heard at an impersonal distance. We knew each other as two people with a story each to tell and a shared commitment that we could work on together.

After about a year of such meetings on a regular basis I felt I had a reasonably solid foundation to build on. I organised meetings three or four times a year, and invited those I had had one-to-ones with. When a new meeting was to be held I would invite those who had responded previously as well as any new people.

It was good that we never managed to find a name for this group. To have named it would have been to narrow it. A solid core of parishioners came regularly, augmented by many more who came when they could, or motivated by whatever we were taking as our topic.

The topic depended on where the parish journey had taken us at any given time. But it was always about recognising and celebrating the strengths of becoming a more relational community, and then taking some action to make it more so.

At the first meeting everyone had agreed that we wanted to be a more relational community where people knew each other and felt they belonged. They were able to make a long list of very good reasons why it didn't happen, which turned into a challenge: Why don't we make it happen?

The strategy came out of a Lent course where a dozen people signed up to be parish visitors and conduct one-to-ones. Parishioners were asked once a month to sign up if they wanted a visit, and were assigned to one of the dozen.

From time to time we would hold a Listening Campaign in conjunction with London Citizens. This would enable one-to-ones to take place across the parish using a variety of strategies with a focus not only on how we made our own community stronger but also how we could participate in London Citizens campaigns to make the wider community a better place, and help convert the culture of our society so that it better reflects the values of the Gospel.

These strategies included house meetings and house Masses; holding refreshments after Mass as a special event over a fixed number of weeks; encouraging some mini one-to-ones during the Mass. At its best the house meeting or Mass was an opportunity to ask someone to be host and see them grow as a leader, as well as putting neighbours together who had previously only been on nodding terms. Over a fixed period of time, these Listening Campaigns brought people together and got them talking to each other, always with an action plan at the end.

A second development came in the attempt to build small neighbourhood groups. Its impetus came from a desire to take the relational culture that had been built in the parish community out onto the streets and neighbourhoods of the parish. To my mind this is vital. A parish that is only concerned with itself will never get very far.

The parish is too large to be realistically called a community: only by forming neighbourhood groups within the parish – those who live within streets of each other – is it possible to effectively establish the sense of belonging that makes a community. Within that group it would be possible to carry out the important work of the parish, like passing on faith to the next generation in ways that would have so much more impact. Equally, problems that develop on the streets can be spotted much earlier and where necessary groups can plug into much bigger alliances to campaign to deal with them. In the end these groups offer myriad ways of letting us be good neighbours to one another.

In time, the relational road simply became the way of doing my ministry and crept into every aspect of parish life. How much easier on so many levels is it to conduct sessions with parents of children preparing for First Communion when someone from the parish has already had a one-to-one conversation with them.

Yet I am staggered by the number of meetings I attend both in the Church and outside that remain task-orientated. How much more would be achieved so much more easily if attention was paid to building relations within the group first, before moving to working together.

I had between two and three hundred full one-to-ones, as well as countless shorter ones, in my time in the parish. They informed and enriched my ministry immeasurably. Indeed I am not sure how it can be possible to preach on a regular basis to a community without such a knowledge of the desires and fears, joys and anxieties, of those who make it up. Yet when my time came to leave I knew many of those conversations and the relationships that went with them would be lost to the parish. It is important that one-to-ones do not take place just between the parish priest and the parishioners, but between the parishioners too.

When I first came to the parish our community organiser had asked me if I could give him a list of twenty leaders in the parish he could meet. I struggled to get ten. By the time I left I could have named fifty without consulting any lists.

When some researchers who wanted to study our experience of relational organising asked to meet some of these leaders, it was a struggle to bring it down to twelve. At the meeting I was largely silent; instead these parishioners spoke of their experience of being Church in that place at that time. Many of my colleagues will know that we priests often speak and wonder if anyone is listening, if anyone gets what we are on about. On that evening, as those people spoke about their community with such pride and passion, I understood for the first time just how much people had not only been listening. I understood the power of relational action, and how, when it is rooted in people's lives, it builds community like nothing else.

The one-to-one meeting – Ed Chambers

So what are one-to-one relational meetings? They are the glue that brings people together and allows them to embrace the tension of living between the world-as-it-is and the world-as-it-should-be. Properly understood, the relational meeting is not a science, not a technique, but an art form in which one spirit goes after another spirit to create connection, confrontation, and an exchange of talent and energy, eventually leading to some kind of joint action. Perhaps one-to-ones would be better named 'the mixing of human spirits.'

The relational meeting is an encounter that is face-to-face and one-to-one. It's purpose is to explore the possibility of a public relationship with another person. Let me stop there. I said a public relationship. This may be one of the biggest causes of misunderstanding and failure regarding relational meetings. We are not looking for new 'friends' when we are conducting a series of one-to-ones. Friendship is something that happens in private life. It usually happens accidentally (a roommate in college, a next-door neighbor, a co-worker), grows slowly over time, is based on many shared experiences, and often lasts a lifetime. Real friendships are few and far between. You are lucky if you have a handful in a lifetime. And, of course, one of those 'friendships' can turn to romance, physical intimacy, and even marriage. And marriage can produce more private relationships in the form of children, grandchildren, in-laws, etc.

None of that is what we are looking for in one-to-ones. The purpose of a systematic, disciplined, organized process of relational meetings is a public relationship – one built on mutual self-interest, respect and power, that eventually leads to joint action. When you are doing one-to-ones, you are searching for energy, insight and a willingness to act and to lead. Where these are present, you will have found some additional strength and talent to add to your public collective, whether that be a citizens organization, a local religious congregation, a political party, or some kind of social movement. Without hundreds of such relational meetings, people cannot forge lasting public relationships that lead to collective action. For the relational meeting is a means to an end. The end is always collective action, and with that kind of power we can change the world.

James Madison said, 'Great things can only be accomplished in a narrow compass.' The relational meeting is that narrow compass – one person face-to-face with another – but significant in intention and purpose. A one-to-one is a small stage that lends itself to acts of memory, imagination and reflection. It constitutes a public conversation on a scale that allows space for thoughts, aspirations, values and talent to mix. It is where public newness begins, and it is the only hope for the long-term survival and triumph of democracy.[8]

Turning a church around: the American organiser's story – Michael Gecan

In the early eighties, a parish in the Bushwick section of Brooklyn joined East Brooklyn Congregations. Its dwindling congregation of 150 members met in a crumbling cavern of a church building in a community that had suffered years of white flight and arson. The building needed hundreds of thousands of dollars in repairs. And the diocese was threatening to shut the doors. When I asked the four staff members –Fr. Ed Brady, Sr. Frances Gritte, Fr. Lew Maynard, and Sr. Maryellen Kane – why they had decided to join the organization, they answered honestly: they felt that they had absolutely nothing to lose and wondered whether they could try to apply the universals of the IAF approach in a last-ditch attempt to disorganize and reorganize the parish.

We met for days, a few miles from the smoldering streets of Bushwick, in the peaceful backyard of Sr. Frances's home in nearby Queens, where an occasional bird twittered at us from up in the trees. I provided training on how to do individual meetings, on the tension between a relational culture and the typical bureaucratic culture we find in most congregations, and on the identification and engagement of talented new leaders. They argued and struggled among themselves as to how they would relate to one another.

They wondered how they would fend off resistance to any new approach from the parish's small but fierce old guard. And they schemed to find ways to finesse the diocese while quietly pursuing this organizational experiment.

At the end of several months of training and strategy, the staff came to a critical decision: everything that they did – beyond liturgy and necessary crisis response – would be put to a simple test. Did the activity lead to the *training and developing of leaders? Or not? If it did, they would invest their time and energy in it. If it did not, they would avoid it, or withdraw from it.*

If you have ever run a parish, business, or agency, you know how radical this decision was. For the parish staff, it meant saying no to the existing groups and cliques that had come to expect a member of the parish staff to sit through three-hour meetings of unbearable boredom. In dying parishes, this practice is rationalized as a 'ministry of presence.'

The staff encouraged veteran leaders to think differently, and individual staff members mentored, supported, and trained key leaders who were open to change. But when entrenched leaders refused to respond, then the staff moved ahead and sought out newer, more open, less 'established' leaders with vision, energy, and a following.

The staff stopped being managers, paper-pushers, baby-sitters, or reactors. They became talent scouts, coaches, teachers, and trainers. They also moved aggressively beyond the walls of the existing parish and sought out the majority of members not yet in the pews. They went into the Hope Gardens housing projects, into the tenements along Central Avenue, into welfare offices, and into public schools. The pastor even visited one of the low-wage knitting mills that employed many of his monolingual, Spanish-speaking members. I walked in with him one morning. The workers were bent over tables overflowing with fabric, intent on their sewing and in fear of the owner. We had heard how he enforced discipline: by brandishing a bolo knife now and then. When the first worker spotted Fr. Brady, her face went from stunned surprise to joy to gratitude, while the expression of the owner, eying us through the glass wall of his office, hardened.

Slowly, after hundreds of individual meetings and scores of house meetings and block meetings, after a phase of direct action on matters of immediate concern, the congregation began to grow. Sunday attendance went from 150 to 400 after about six months of work. Then, six months later, 800 began to worship. Then 1,000. Then, after two years, nearly 1,500 people refilled the large, ornate, crumbling Catholic church. The diocese responded by committing to fund the renovation of the church building. Artisans repaired the roof, patched holes, and repainted the gold leaf in the vault over the altar.

The pastor, largely unrecognized for his remarkable work, was quietly transferred. One by one, the other staff members moved on. A determined and experienced new duo, Msgr. John Powis and Sr. Kathy Maire, took over and kept pushing the parish forward. St. Barbara's is now vital, teeming, complicated, and challenging –central to a community hungry for a stable institution that can effectively anchor neighborhood life.[9]

Focus on *Quadragesimo Anno* (1931)

- Issued on the fortieth anniversary of *Rerum Novarum*, *Quadragesimo Anno* recalls and develops four themes from Leo's encyclical, confirming the Church's solidarity with workers, condemning the widening gap between rich and poor, clarifying the duties of labour and capital, and setting forth a path for the 'reconstruction of the social order' in the wake of the Wall Street Crash of 1929.
- The political tensions at the time were strong. Relations between the Vatican and Mussolini were increasingly strained as the dictator moved towards totalitarianism, suppressing Catholic organisations which sought to remain independent of the state. Catholic Action, a mass organisation of ordinary Catholics, set out to infuse the public spheres with the values of Catholic social action, offering an alternative to both liberalism and the totalitarianism of both Left and Right.
- The author was mainly a Jesuit, Oswald von Nell-Breuning, although sections 91–96 in support of syndicalism were written by the Pope himself.

Subsidiarity– 'Reconstructing the social order'

- The encyclical's main purpose is 'the re-establishment of a truly Christian social order'. Pius observes that the State has become far too over-extended because it has had to take responsibility for what was formerly done by civil-society institutions. But these have been destroyed and weakened by free-market individualism:

> When we speak of the reform of institutions it is principally the State that we have in mind. Not indeed that all salvation is to be hoped for from its intervention, but because on account of the evil of 'individualism', as we called it, things have come to such a pass that the highly developed social life, which once flourished in a variety of prosperous and interdependent institutions, has been damaged and all but ruined, leaving virtually only individuals and the State, with little harm to the latter. But the State, deprived of a supporting social structure, and now encumbered with all the burdens once borne by disbanded associations, is in consequence overwhelmed and submerged by endless affairs and responsibilities. (*QA* 78)

- This is wrong, for 'one should not withdraw from individuals and commit to the community what they can accomplish by their own enterprise and industry' (*QA* 79). 'Just as it is gravely wrong to take from individuals what they can accomplish by their own initiative and industry and give it to the community, so also it is an injustice and at the same time a grave evil and disturbance of right order to assign to a greater and higher association what lesser and subordinate organizations can do.' The more this principle of subsidiarity – the principle of civil society – is followed, 'the more excellent will be the authority and efficacy of society, and the happier and more prosperous will be the condition of the commonwealth' (*QA* 80).

- Pius XI then proposes means to overcome the current social divisions between opposing classes. He suggests groupings called 'Orders', which have certain features of medieval guilds. The specifics of what he proposes are less important than the principles behind it: that the health of a society lies in the strength of its civil-society institutions, and that it is principally through these that the common good is articulated.

> The public institutions of the nations should be such as to make all human society conform to the requirements of the common good, that is, the norm of social justice. If this is done, that very important part of social life, the economic system, will of necessity be restored to sanity and right order. (*QA* 110)

4 ASSEMBLING IN SOLIDARITY

There were so many different people, from different backgrounds.
There were so many from ethnic minority groups. It was great to
see everybody, sitting there together with one mind, with one idea.
You don't get that all the time ... I felt good about the evening
because I found myself thinking, 'What did I just come from? I just
came from something that could be part of history.' I was running
on adrenalin!

Tony, parishioner at Our Lady and St George's parish

Some people don't quite 'get' London Citizens until they attend one of its
big public assemblies. Before they arrive, they're not quite sure what
they've agreed to. Even the word *assembly* is unfamiliar. A conference? No:
people speak for no more than a few minutes, and there are no papers or
talks. A debate? No: there are no motions, although consent is sometimes
sought for a particular sort of action. A hustings? No. Hustings are where
politicians lay out their agendas and ask us to support them, whereas
politicians who come to London Citizens assemblies are asked to support
our agenda. And sometimes they have to sit through powerful testimonies
by undocumented migrants, or cleaners on minimum wages, or people
burdened by unfair interest rates, which is certainly not what they would
have planned for a hustings.

They're also surprised to find it's not all talk. London Citizens assemblies include choirs, 'Greek choruses' and drama performances. Citizen
politics is serious, but that doesn't stop it being entertaining and fun.

Across London in most boroughs there are town halls, mostly dating
back to the nineteenth century – some of them very pretty, in a gaudy sort
of way. They are where 'the people' used to gather to call for action or ask
politicians to agree to something. But TV and the media have put paid to
that. Nowadays, they are mostly used for weddings and corporate conferences. But London Citizens hires them for the older purpose – raising not
a few eyebrows in the process.

Most years, London Citizens' chapters – East, South and West London
– hold autumn assemblies, attended by a thousand or so people. But
occasionally they come together to hold a London-wide assembly, when
the numbers double.

Politicians who are invited to them often ask, 'How many will be there?' They might be hoping for a few dozen, if they're lucky – the kinds of numbers MPs usually address. When they hear '2,500 people' they fall off their chairs.

The word *assembly* comes from the Greek word *ekklesia* from which we get the word 'church'. It is a 'civic congregation' where people of different faiths and none who live alongside each other express the hopes and frustrations they share for the city, commit to working in solidarity with each other for the common good, and hold people with power to account. All are participants: everyone takes a role, if only to raise a hand confirming support for a decision. Like powerful liturgy, an assembly offers every person in the room a vivid and memorable experience, one which teaches in action the ideals of citizen organising and in doing so moves people to a new hope of moving 'the world as it is' towards 'the world as it should be'.

Focus on *Gaudium et Spes*

- One of the four major 'constitutions' of the Second Vatican Council, *Gaudium et Spes* signalled a dramatic turning of the Church's pastoral care towards the world as a whole, after more than a century of exclusion from public life at the hands of the secular liberal state and atheistic totalitarianism. It famously begins with a leitmotif of its whole message of solidarity: 'The joys and the hopes, the grief and anguish of the people of our time, especially those who are poor and afflicted, are the joys and hopes, the griefs and anguish of the followers of Christ' (GS 1).

- The document makes a new contribution to CST by grounding its arguments on theology as well as natural law. It is the most authoritative and significant document of CST, even though it is not one of the five *Rerum Novarum* anniversary encyclicals.

- *Gaudium et Spes* makes clear that the Church is concerned with all human struggles for a life with dignity, building the solidarity of the human community, and with the humanisation of human work in the face of the depersonalising forces of the market. It argues that the disciples of Christ must be especially concerned with building up solidarity, for human dignity can only be attained in community with others; hence the need of an ethic of justice and equality which is rooted in participation in community.

- The document was released against the background of the civil rights protests in the US, as well as the Cold War, and many independence movements in the developing world. It was a time of unprecedented prosperity, and optimism about human rights. *Gaudium et Spes* sought to provide a Christian framework for these movements for change.

Whatever its purpose and scale – chapter or London-wide – London Citizens assemblies are an opportunity for the diverse groups and communities who are members of a citizens' organisation, or who are joining, to *pledge commitment* to the whole and to *recognise one another* as part of that alliance. The evening is a *celebration* of their unity and power; it is designed to make us more powerful than we were. Third, it expresses the shared *vision* and the *values* held in common, thereby teaching members and guests alike why we work together, and for what purpose. Fourth, the actual problems (e.g. poor wages, street crime, housing) that a citizens' organisation is working to address through its campaigns will be introduced by people who tell stories and give *testimony* from their own experience. Fifth, during the evening members will try to *secure public agreements* with people from the business community and in elected office who have been invited to attend. Sixth, there will be *votes*, a show of hands, and sometimes people will be asked to caucus before coming to a decision. When it is over, the organisers and leaders involved in the assembly's preparation will gather for an *evaluation*. They will ask: what business did we set out to do? Did we do it? Are we stronger? What could we have done better?

The main work is beforehand. Preparing for a tightly run 90-minute citizens' assembly takes many weeks and will involve dozens of people from the diverse parishes and local organisations whose people fill the hall on the night.

There are four chief characteristics which make a citizens' assembly unlike any other night out.[1]

1   A full hall doesn't just happen

A full hall signals commitment and passion; above all, it signals *power* – the legitimacy of a citizen organisation's claim to be representing significant opinion. It is much easier to persuade a politician or banker to say 'yes' if you ask them to do so on a stage in a packed town hall, with thousands clapping and cheering. A packed assembly instantly creates an atmosphere charged with possibility.

That's why a lot of work goes into that turnout – meetings, phone calls, emails and reminder text messages. Member institutions will be asked to give quotas – the teams will commit to bringing certain numbers, and those numbers of seats will be allocated to that institution. This is where the one-to-ones pay off. An institution which has invested time in one-to-ones already has the 'spiritual energy' to summon people out of their homes. People come, because they know it's important; because leaders and organisers have done one-to-ones, they know it's important to the people they call.

Institutions with strong relationships produce the best turnout. Member organisations vary in size greatly, from small Nonconformist congregations and ethnic associations to large Catholic parishes and mosques. The quotas given reflect, obviously, these differences in size; but in practice, levels of turnout rarely mirror the size of an institution's membership. Time and again, the groups who produce the lion's share of turnout are those with the strongest internal relationships.

> ... having the politicians actually having to think about our questions and mull them over and produce answers on the spot without circumventing as they tend to do ... was excellent.
>
> Mary Grisdale, St Antony's, Forest Gate

2 Recognising the people

After music and the reading of a reflection, a citizens' assembly begins with a 'roll-call' of the member groups present. This takes time: 15, maybe 20 minutes. For many it is the most memorable part of the evening. As each representative of each member institution explains why their community, parish or group is joining or recommitting to the alliance, it generates a feeling of excitement and joy: ordinary people – Christians of all denominations, alongside Muslims and Sikhs and Jews, and people of no faith – working in solidarity for the common good generates a strong sense of the 'world as it should be'. Civil society – its power and its energy – is made visible.

Each person has just a few seconds in turn at the podium on stage. They introduce their people (often asking for a cheer from the floor from their group), hand over a cheque for a year's membership dues, and offer a brief word on the reasons for their participation and contribution.

That cheque is important. Its size will vary, depending on the size of the institution, but it says two important things: first, that this is an alliance of organisations which belongs to the organisations themselves: the organisers are accountable to the institutions which make up London Citizens. Second, the dues cheque indicates that London Citizens is independent: a self-sustaining, autonomous civil-sector organisation. London Citizens accepts no money from government or political parties or corporations. Its freedom of movement is not restricted by ties of obligation to the holders of the power London Citizens wishes to make accountable. London Citizens is 'organised people and organised money' – its *own* people; its *own* money.

The dues are not enough: the costs of the organisation's salaries and administration come mostly from charitable grants from trusts. But charitable trusts only invest in London Citizens because they see that the member institutions are willing to do so.

Only member institutions can join. People take part via the institution. This is by design. Individuals, like active leaders, come and go, but the institutions remain rooted in the local community and in the values and vision which sustain them.

Community organising begins from the premise that these institutions – congregations, union branches, ethnic associations, tenants groups – are the pillars of a healthy democracy. It is in them that people first develop what Sheldon Wolin calls 'politicalness' – 'our capacity for developing into beings who know and value what it means to participate in and be responsible for the care and improvement of our common and collective life'.[2]

3   Run by the people, for the people

That's why London Citizens' assemblies are co-chaired by a small team of three or four leaders from member organisations. In addition to keeping the meeting to the evening's agenda, their role is to maintain the engagement and consent of members in the assembly hall, and to interpret and teach from the politics of the evening.

The co-chairs will often be members of the advisory group of a London Citizens chapter – local leaders who will be involved in the preparation for an assembly, meeting several times with their organiser to develop the agenda, put together a script for different sections of the evening, and figure out how best to pin down the invited business and political guests.

Assemblies will always have a timekeeper who sits on stage with the co-chairs. Armed with a bell, the timekeeper curbs speakers who overrun – whether guests, members, or the co-chairs themselves. No one is exempt from the bell. An efficient, well-run assembly which starts and ends on time is crucial to demonstrating the organisation's competence. And it respects the fact that in the modern city people's time is precious. People who come to London Citizens assemblies trust the organisers not to keep them beyond the advertised time.

> *We've got to get back to our humanity. This is what we've introduced ourselves to with London Citizens. Can you believe the Roman Catholic people, the Anglican church people, and the Muslims together? I can't believe it! It never happens!*
>
> Roland Biosah, trade union leader

4   Power before programme

There are three basic criteria for evaluating an assembly: did we develop leaders? Did we secure agreements which move our campaigns forward? Did we build our power for the future?

Although a BBO such as London Citizens is known for its victories on issues such as wages and housing, it is more than a vehicle for winning campaigns. There is a community organising maxim: 'power precedes programme'. When people have the opportunity to grow and develop as leaders, the power of the organisation is built. People learn in the formal one-day, two-day and five-day trainings put on by London Citizens each year; but the place where that learning is put into practice and absorbed is in action and in the assemblies.

> *Great care must be taken about civic and political formation, which is of the utmost necessity today for the population as a whole, and especially for youth, so that all citizens can play their part in the life of the political community.* (GS 75)

The one leading the evaluation will first ask: 'How do we feel?' If the assembly has gone well, people will respond with words like 'encouraged' and 'inspired' – a sure sign that the assembly has been permeated with that quality of love Pope Benedict spoke of in urging a politics of solidarity. We've done a little of God's work.

The assembly offers people memorable chances to test and surprise themselves. Speaking on stage in front of hundreds of others – whether giving a testimony, proposing a new campaign, or pressing a politician – is both nerve-wracking and exhilarating. Even for those who are sitting in the body of the hall, there is real appreciation that the assembly is giving new people a chance to be leaders in public. Part of the evaluation is to salute those who took part, to congratulate them on taking forward the agenda which makes a difference. In this way, ordinary people learn their politicalness – that, with others, they can make a difference, working for the common good of all in collaboration with others.

> *You see people around you being prominent in society, making a real difference and you think that's great but I could never do that. That assembly made me realise that there are stepping stones to getting to that stage.*
>
> Kathleen, school student

The public business of an assembly – the doing of deals to move campaigns forward – is critical to its success or otherwise. People will have their own judgements on this, but there is usually consensus afterwards on whether the politicians and business leaders were handled too harshly or too leniently – or indeed with real skill – by the co-chairs and the campaign team members; and whether the expected deals were done. Did the politician prove slippery, or did we get a firm 'yes' or 'no' to what he was asked? What exactly did he commit to? However much preparation and forethought goes into it, there is real unpredictability in a citizens' assembly – and that's the part which gets people talking afterwards.

> *The kids were excited by it. They were asking the following day, what do you think of this, what do you think of that. They had made opinions already from such a short exposure.*
>
> Rosa, teacher at Trinity Catholic High School

Finally the one leading the evaluation will ask: 'Are we more powerful as a result of this assembly?' Power is the 'capacity to act', the ability to bring about change. The type of power a BBO builds is relational power, the power generated when people peacefully connect with each other across social and other boundaries to build the common good.

If the room was full, we are certainly halfway there. If members spoke with passion and with clarity, this will help. If the organisation was recognised and respected by invited guests, and better still if these guests publicly committed to agreements being sought, this too will give people a great sense of belonging to an organisation with power.

In Lord Acton's famous dictum, 'Power tends to corrupt; absolute power corrupts absolutely'. Christians are justifiably cautious about power. But *powerlessness* is equally a problem, as the American Protestant theologian Reinhold Niebuhr understood. 'Power without love is tyranny,' he once wrote; 'but love without power is sentimentality.' Martin Luther King, in his address to the Southern Christian Leadership Conference (1967), showed that he too understood this:

> Power properly understood is nothing but the ability to achieve purpose. It is the strength required to bring about social, political and economic change ... What is needed is a realization that power without love is reckless and abusive, and love without power is sentimental and anaemic. Power at its best is love implementing the demands of justice, and justice at its best is power correcting everything that stands against love.

We each have God-given power. CST invites us not to deny that power but to use it creatively and with perseverance for the common good. A citizens' assembly is an attempt to live out that challenging instruction, bringing many together in solidarity, building an 'ability to achieve purpose' – the power to bring about change.

Let's see how London Citizens did that at its most recent assembly – in the heart of the City of London.

The London Citizens Autumn Assembly, 25 November 2009

That night 2,000 – that's how many the place could seat – gathered at the Barbican Centre in the City, London's financial district.

The choice of venue was significant. The main business of the evening was to persuade politicians and bankers to agree to an agenda drawn up over many months, under the title, 'Taking responsibility in the economic crisis', at the centre of which was a call for a cap on interest rates. The people were assembled in the heart of the global capital to hold financial power to account.

After a music performance, two cocky young compères, 'Ashley J and Tee-J' –former students of one of the member schools of TELCO – acted as a kind of Greek Chorus. 'What is this assembly about, Tee-J?', asks Ashley. Tee-J goes over to a man in a suit at the podium, Dr Luke

Bretherton, a parishioner at St Paul's Church in Hammersmith. Behind him are seated the religious leaders who will later read together from Scripture.

'So who are you?' Tee-J asks him.

'We are 2,000 gathered here, representing over 150 institutions, who in turn represent over 50,000 people from across this city,' Luke answers. 'We are people who take responsibility for ourselves, our families and the communities where we live. And we expect others to do the same, whether they be neighbours, bankers or politicians.'

'I like, I like,' says Tee-J, grinning. 'So what *is* London Citizens' response to the economic crisis?'

> *Along with cultural, economic and social development, there is a growing desire among many people to play a greater part in organizing the life of the political community. In the conscience of many arises an increasing concern that the rights of minorities be recognized, without any neglect for their duties toward the political community. In addition, there is a steadily growing respect for men of other opinions or other religions. At the same time, there is wider cooperation to guarantee the actual exercise of personal rights to all citizens, and not only to a few privileged individuals.* (GS 73)

'We've been working with low-paid workers across London for the past decade getting them a living wage,' said Luke. 'We've spent time listening to what the impact of the recession has been on them – we've had a thousand one-to-ones and about a hundred house meetings. From that experience of listening to people we've formulated the proposals that you're going to hear tonight. And that process came together at the end of September when a couple of dozen people came together to draw up those proposals. They were then voted on at delegates' assemblies in east, West and South London – more than 700 people in total voted on them, representing our 150 institutions. These proposals were not born out of any ideology or political programme; they were born out of listening to ordinary people, and working together for the common good.'

'Tee-J, you're looking a bit confused,' says Ashley. 'Let me break it down for you east-end, like. Basically, people here tonight are putting their trust back in democracy, getting people together to decide what they want to happen, and putting them back to the people, what have the power to change these things.'

'Oh, I get it now,' says Tee-J, to applause. 'So what are your aims?' he asks Luke.

'The thread running through these five proposals', he answers, 'is the need to rebalance the power of money, which for too long has dominated where we live and how we live, with the power of ordinary people. What we're calling for tonight is responsibility from our bankers and our political leaders, and the need for better structures for borrowing and lending.'

'So why', asks Tee-J, 'is tonight so important?'

'Tonight, above other nights, is important for London Citizens,' Luke answers. 'It marks the launch of a campaign we're taking up to the General Election. We're calling tonight on bankers and politicians to find out where they stand in relation to what we're proposing. They might say no. That's OK. That just cuts out for us our work. We know as London Citizens we have to organise and work together for any real change to happen. We're here to find out who our allies are, and what work we have to do.'

Then the chairs introduce themselves, and various sister organisations are introduced – from Germany, the US, and citizens' groups in Oxford, Cambridge and Milton Keynes – and asked to stand up. Journalists, trade union leaders, funders and others who help London Citizens are also name-called and asked to stand and be recognised. Then the roll-call of London Citizens members begins: one person from each borough calls out the names of the institutions present, and there is rapturous applause. On a screen behind, the boroughs are filled in as their members' names are called. It looks like an invading army.

Another chair then invites up a number of immigrant organisations who have taken part in the 'Strangers into Citizens' campaign calling for a regularisation of undocumented migrants who have put down roots in the UK. In a few sentences, each of them says what the campaign has meant to them, and how desperate they are to 'step out of the shadows and into a normal life'.

Before the main matter of the evening, there is some business to be done with the Mayor, Boris Johnson. Patsy Cummings, a leader from South London, recalls the 2008 London Citizens mayoral assembly, when the four mayoral candidates were asked to sign up to an agenda which included regularisation of undocumented migrants and the living wage.

To the amazement of the media, Boris agreed to both, and has since had a warm relationship with London Citizens. He had been nervous at the 2008 assembly, admitting on stage that this was the most 'awesome and terrifying' gathering of his election campaign. But tonight, after more than a year and many meetings with London Citizens leaders – including an event the week before when he declared City Hall the 200th Safe Haven – he is on bullish form, oozing charm and wit. He congratulates London Citizens for the 'brilliant way, and may I say ruthless way, in which you bend us politicians to your will, and you get us to deliver on the good things that we both believe in'. He promises to look at the Community Land Trust proposal and lists recent achievements – 'at your urging and your inspiration' – including his advocacy of CitySafe havens – and the London Living Wage (LLW), which the previous summer he had set at £7.60 an hour (compared to the national minimum wage of £5.80), congratulating the many companies – PwC, KPMG, Linklaters, Barclays Bank – who are 'supporting a measure that makes practical business sense; it not only helps to knit the loyalty of your staff and thereby to save on your employment costs, it is, of course, the compassionate thing to do.'

The London Citizens Mayoral Aaccountability Assembly, 9 April 2008

Looking out over the crowd at the London Citizens 'mayoral accountability assembly' on the evening of 9 April, it was clear that an extraordinary event was taking place. Westminster Central Hall was packed to the rafters – 2,500 people in all, throbbing with energy and self-confidence as the roll of over a hundred organisations that make up the membership of London Citizens was called out. People of all ages and backgrounds, from faith communities, schools, union branches, residents' associations, voluntary groups and ethnic organisations stood and cheered as their organisations' names were called out.

The event had been billed by many in the press as a hustings but it was quite the opposite of a traditional hustings at which it is the candidates and their parties that set the agenda. At the accountability assembly, London Citizens demanded that the candidates respond to their priorities. 'If the mayoral candidates want our votes on 1 May, they have to prove their worth by signing up to our agenda and implementing it when in office,' said Sarfraz Jeraj, one of the assembly co-chairs and a community leader from South London.

One of the criticisms sometimes levelled at London Citizens is that it has only a veneer of democracy. 'I've noticed,' says Jane Holgate, a long-time observer of the organisation, 'that trade unionists who have attended London Citizens assemblies for the first time – and who are not members – are alarmed that there is no debate, no motions, no amendments and no speeches from the floor, so they conclude that it is undemocratic.'

The assemblies are indeed staged, but that is because they are not decision-making bodies. Assemblies are showcases of work done and planned and an opportunity to present a united front to public figures who are being called to account on behalf of the communities in the room. The real voting and democratic decision-making takes place at dozens of smaller meetings, in borough caucuses, action teams, strategy groups, delegate assemblies, trustees and within the communities that make up London Citizens.

The mayoral assembly is a case in point. For six months, London Citizens members had been engaged in a 'listening campaign', holding meetings in school canteens, church halls and neighbours' front rooms to discuss the issues that mattered most to them. Member institutions were asked to find ways to encourage as many people as possible to answer the simple question, 'What would you like the next mayor of London to do for you and your family and neighbourhood?'

London Citizens provided workshops, questionnaires and a DVD to help the groups organise their discussions, but communities were given a free hand to run their listening campaigns as they felt best. At St Margaret's church in Canning Town, for example, a team of ten women each pledged to speak to ten other parishioners, as well as going round to all the small gatherings where church members normally came together.

To build their confidence, people at St Margaret's were asked what changes they wanted to see in the parish, as well as the wider city. They understood that all of the issues raised would be pursued at one level or another, even if they did not get prioritised for the mayoral assembly. So besides engaging people in the wider political process, the listening campaign created openings for people to participate more actively in their own communities.

> Around 50,000 people ultimately took part in the listening
> campaign. Hundreds of ideas came from the grassroots, with the
> most popular proposals being debated and voted on by a city-wide
> delegates' assembly. Out of that process came the Citizens Agenda,
> which candidates were asked to sign up to, including measures to
> make London a safer, fairer, better-housed and more welcoming
> city.
>
> And sign up they did. With some minor caveats on detail, the
> candidates agreed to all of London Citizens' proposals – including
> support for the regularisation of migrant workers, which is not the
> party policy of either the Tories or Labour. Perhaps London
> Citizens' ability to push candidates beyond the usual party policies
> was a reflection of the power gathered in the room that night, and
> the growing influence of London Citizens generally. It is a power
> that derives from their very different way of doing politics.
>
> Deborah Littman[3]

The Mayor then praises the Strangers into Citizens earned amnesty proposal which he has championed since London Citizens persuaded him of it before the mayoral election in 2008.[4] 'We have led the way', he said to applause, 'in proposing an earned amnesty for people who have been here for a long time, in this city, because I believe if they have been here for a long time and if they can show they are good citizens and loyal to this country and its institutions, we should enable them to express their loyalty and their love; and number two, because it makes simple economic sense for them to enter the system and pay their taxes like everybody else. And that is why I am working with my colleagues and with my political opponents we are championing the earned amnesty, and I believe it deserves wider national consideration.'

Boris then warns bankers thinking of 'hauling down great stonking bonuses' at Christmas to remember Ebenezer Scrooge, 'who lent money at usurious rates to the subprime sector of Victorian London' and who achieved redemption by giving away his money to those who needed it.

The Mayor having recommitted to working with London Citizens, the 'economic responsibility' agenda begins with leading representatives of employers in London taking the podium to praise the LLW. Barclays, KPMG, PwC and Linklaters are enthusiastic about its business and moral benefits. They salute London Citizens, and explain how they had insisted on the LLW not just for their employees but also for their subcontractors.

'Working and travelling in London is expensive, and if you're on a low wage it's proportionately more expensive,' Oonagh Harpur of Linklaters told the assembly. 'This is the right thing to do.'

Next up is Cllr Lutfur Rahman, leader of Tower Hamlets Council, who says all his full-time and agency staff are on the LLW. 'When I was growing up, my father's generation did several jobs to make ends meet, and it is a travesty that in modern London people are still earning poverty wages,' he says.

A photoshoot follows, with the Mayor presenting LLW awards to the employers. The City Parochial Foundation announces a £700,000 award to London Citizens to fund the expansion of the LLW over the next four years. 'For us that money is well spent,' says the Foundation's chair.

Then comes the tension.

Steve, a cleaner who works for the Corporation of London, describes how he earns £6.76 an hour before deductions, and how he and his fellow workers need to work extra hours after a nine-hour shift to pay for the costs of bringing up children.

Cllr Mark Boleat, of the Corporation of London, is invited onto the stage. 'Because we are neighbours and share the same economic crisis,' the chair, Junaid Ahmed, tells him, 'will you join hands with Tower Hamlets Council and the finance houses we have met here tonight, and make the City of London a living-wage employer?'

Boleat looks uncomfortable. He responds that all those employed directly by the Corporation are paid at least the LLW, but this was not the case with agency and contracted staff – 'in common with all local authorities, bar one or two'. But he promises to review his procurement contracts, and to work with London Citizens. A relationship is forged.

It is less than a commitment to the LLW, but a remarkable step forward: Boleat had reacted angrily to London Citizens leaders when they first approached him, rejecting the very principle of the LLW. Now, at least, he is agreeing to review it—under pressure from the size of the audience, and from the knowledge that one of the poorest boroughs in London (Tower Hamlets) pays the LLW, but not the world's wealthiest local authority. By appearing on stage and making that promise, he has *recognised* London Citizens and is making himself *accountable* to it. It has been by such steps – converting angry refusals into public commitments to a relationship – that the London Citizens LLW campaign has put lifted more than 5,000 working families out of poverty.

> *Both the regulation of the financial sector, so as to safeguard weaker parties and discourage scandalous speculation, and experimentation with new forms of finance, designed to support development projects, are positive experiences that should be further explored and encouraged, highlighting the responsibility of the investor ... This is all the more necessary in these days when financial difficulties can become severe for many of the more vulnerable sectors of the population, who should be protected from the risk of usury and from despair. The weakest members of society should be helped to defend themselves against usury, just as poor peoples should be helped to derive real benefit from micro-credit, in order to discourage the exploitation that is possible in these two areas.*
>
> Pope Benedict XVI, *Caritas in Veritate* 65

After a performance by one of the member schools, the next three London Citizens proposals – a financial literacy programme for schools, investment in mutual lending, and a statutory charter for responsible lending – are spelled out, and more relationships forged on stage. Agnesa, an east European parishioner at one of the member churches in West London Citizens, who used to work night shifts, shares her story of the crippling debt she can no longer manage after losing her job, and the threats from bailiffs and debt-collection agencies which followed her fruitless efforts to speak to her bank manager. 'There are days when I do not want to leave the house, days when I don't want to carry on,' she says in a calm, clear voice. 'But there comes a time when you have to stand up and say "enough is enough". My name is Agnesa, and I want my life back.'

The 20 per cent cap on interest rates is then introduced – by faith leaders together reading from Scripture. A rabbi, a Methodist minister, a Salvation Army officer, the head of the Muslim Council of Britain, and a Catholic monsignor read together from Nehemiah 5:3–13, a story of how an assembly of the people shamed usurers, demanding they give back the ransomed fields and corn.

> *No limits? That's right. Payday lenders charge £25 a month on a £100 loan; that's nearly 300% APR. The sky is the limit for 'sub-prime' lenders who target the 9m people in the UK denied access to credit from banks, mostly in households on very low*

> *incomes who struggle to cover their families' basic needs. Sub-prime lending, worth £35bn a year, bleeds the poorest.*
>
> *The relative silence from faith leaders on this subject is odd. The financial crash has led to a good deal of hand-wringing about bonuses and free-market idolatry; some soul-searching has been spotted at 'money and morality' meetings behind closed doors at Lambeth Palace; or between Catholic bishops and financiers at Schroders Bank, as well as in discussions at St Paul's Cathedral. But that old Biblical sin called usury has seldom disturbed these gatherings, despite an explicit injunction in Pope Benedict XVI's recent encyclical, where usury is mentioned alongside despair. Caritas in Veritate is plain on the topic: the poorest members of society should be protected from loan-sharking, licensed or not, and have access to microcredit …*
>
> *Usury in modern Britain is a scandal comparable to exploitative wages in Victorian days: it was argued then that people who freely enter into a contract should be bound by it. But popes and bishops said otherwise. A desperate person does not enter into such arrangements freely; there is such a thing as a 'just wage' – sufficient to cover basic needs – whatever the market determines. So it is with debt. Plunging the poor into destitution through usury is serious sin. Will the bishops re-discover their inner prophet, set their face against the usurers, and call for regulation? Nehemiah had the idea: 'And I set a great assembly against them.'"[5]*

'This is the heart of the evening,' begins Dr Maurice Glasman, a Jewish leader from East London, citing the Bible, Aristotle, Adam Smith and John Maynard Keynes against usury. 'The issue that confronts us is that money has become much too powerful in our city,' he says, reminding people that the taxpayer bailout of banks in crisis was the largest transfer of wealth from the poor to the rich since William the Conqueror. 'Only organized people can resist the power of money,' he adds. 'We've got to lay down a political limit to how much the rich can exploit the poor in their distress.' This is the beginning of the first anti-usury campaign in 500 years, he continues. 'The living wage raises the floor, the interest rate lowers the ceiling – we've got to win this.'

Another London Citizens leader, a Methodist minister in Hammersmith, pays tribute to Rabbi Nathan Asmoucha, who lost his job at Bevis Marks Synagogue after he allowed London Citizens to meet there for the launch of their anti-usury campaign. 'We salute you for the leadership and courage you have shown', says the Revd Madeleine Andrews, before introducing a Methodist minister from the US, who presents Rabbi Asmoucha with a cheque. 'When we heard that Rabbi Asmoucha had lost his job, we took up a collection,' she said. 'God is with you, justice prevails,' says the Revd Carletta Allen in rousing preacher tones, as the hall gets to its feet to applaud.

'I wonder if you remember how many people told us it was impossible,' says the next speaker at the podium, the Revd Angus Ritchie, an East End priest. He is recalling the start of the LLW campaign. 'But we had faith, we did our research, and look what we've been able to deliver. With this campaign, too, we've built our power, and here is the research ... Change must come. Change can come. And now we ask our politicians: are you going to work with us to make sure change does come?'

One by one, MPs from the three main parties come to the podium to respond to the five proposals, promising to work with London Citizens, giving a variety of responses, and being asked by the chair to clarify and make specific pledges. A series of concessions are extracted, which London Citizens leaders will be able to follow up. The work for the next year is cut out.

The assembly ends with a huge choir on stage. Another London Citizens campaign is launched. We are more powerful. And 2,000 people leave the Barbican clapping and swinging their hips. They feel good.

CST and the call to participation

1   '[I]t belongs to the laity, without waiting passively for orders and directives, to take the initiatives freely and to infuse a Christian spirit into the mentality, customs, laws and structures of the community in which they live' (*OA* 48).

2   'It is up to these Christian communities, with the help of the Holy Spirit, in communion with the bishops who hold responsibility and in dialogue with the other Christian brethren and all people of goodwill, to discern the options and commitments which are called for in order to bring about the social, political, and economic changes seen in many cases to be urgently needed' (*OA* 4).

3   'It is necessary that all participate, each according to his position and role, in promoting the common good. This obligation is inherent in the dignity of the human person ... As far as possible citizens should take an active part in public life' (*CCC* 1913–15).

4   'The direct duty to work for a just ordering of society is proper to the
      lay faithful' (*DCE* 29).
5   'In the Catholic tradition, responsible citizenship is a virtue, and
      participation in political life is a moral obligation ... We are called to
      bring together our principles and our political choices, our values
      and our votes, to help build a better world ... Forming their con-
      sciences in accord with Catholic teaching, Catholic lay women and
      men can become actively involved: running for office; working
      within political parties; communicating their concerns and positions
      to elected officials; and joining diocesan social mission or advocacy
      networks, state Catholic conference initiatives, community organiza-
      tions, and other efforts to apply authentic moral teaching in the
      public square' (US Conference of Catholic Bishops, *Forming Con-
      sciences for Faithful Citizenship*, 13–16).

Focus on *Octogesima Adveniens*

- This 1971 apostolic letter celebrates the eightieth anniversary of
  Rerum Novarum. It was written to Cardinal Maurice Roy, president
  of the newly established Pontifical Commission for Justice and Peace,
  who is the document's main author. Many see *Octogesima Adveniens*
  as Pope Paul VI responding to the Latin American bishops meeting in
  Medellín.
- It is addressed directly to Catholics, urging them to take a greater
  responsibility for the societies in which they lived. *Octogesima Adveniens* emphasises that action for justice is a personal responsibility of
  every Christian, exercised through Christian organisations and institutions, but working with other Christians and all people of goodwill.
- Its major contribution to CST was its insistence that 'the dignity of
  human beings and their ongoing humanisation require a universal
  participation in politics broadly understood, specifically in participation in decision-making towards the common good'.[6]
- The document represents two significant shifts in perspective. Paul
  VI urges the Church in each place to analyse for itself the social
  situation, and to develop programmes to improve it – local solutions
  to local problems. Second, the document embraces 'politics' as a
  means of solving questions. A distinctive feature of the encyclical is
  the emphasis on action: 'the need is felt to pass from economics to
  politics ... each man feels that in the social and economic field, both

national and international, the ultimate decision rests with political power' (OA46).

- The call to politics in *Octogesima Adveniens* is essentially a recognition of the new pluralism which should mark Christian engagement with the public sphere. Gone is the old model of Catholic Action, in which lay people act under the orders of their local bishops to defend the rights of the Church; gone, too, is the suspicion of democratic politics which was never far from papal pronouncements through the nineteenth and early twentieth centuries. The Pope is here calling on Catholics to work with others, in their own right, to change the world. 'In *OA* the Catholic layperson was instead urged to claim an active and independently chosen role in transforming the world in the direction of justice through collaborative action.'[7]

- There are also some new themes. One is urbanisation: Paul VI sees people facing a new loneliness as a result of the anonymity of the city, exacerbated by poverty, indifference and consumerism – a new world of the haves and have-nots – in which exploitation thrives. Another is the environment: the Pope calls for a new sense of responsibility in the management of the earth's resources, in order to provide for all. There is also a more explicit assertion of the option for the poor, in which the poor are not just recipients of justice, but are called to be its agents too.

Key points

1 *Octogesima Adveniens* identifies new social problems: urbanisation, discrimination, emigration. He notes the desire for equality and participation (OA 22–41), which are 'two forms of man's dignity and freedom' (OA 22). The two are related, in that participation in decision-making implies a degree of equality, an equality which Paul VI saw as rooted in the dignity of God-created human beings.

2 Paul VI goes on to address the failed promises of ideologies, and the ambiguous nature of progress, which is often defined in too narrow a materialist sense. Christians must address these problems (OA 42–7), forging a politics of the common good, and allowing political action to express the contemporary demand for greater share in responsibility and decision-making.

3 Participation goes hand in hand with responsibility: 'The quality and truth of human relations, the degree of participation and responsibility, are no less significant and important for the future of society than the quantity and variety of the goods produced and consumed' (*OA* 41).

4   *Octogesima Adveniens* also deals with the search for adequate demo-
    cratic models which will allow for 'a reasonable sharing in responsi-
    bility and in decisions' and 'the giving of wider participation in
    working out decisions, making choices and putting them into prac-
    tice'. This participation, says Paul VI, is 'the path to (a person's)
    development'.

5   Finally, Paul VI issues a call to action (*OA* 48–52) to each Christian,
    calling on them to consider how best they can participate in action.

5 A JUST WAGE IS A LIVING WAGE

'I look forward to the day when we can say that no Londoner is being paid less than the London Living Wage.'

Boris Johnson, mayoral candidate, speaking at the London Citizens Mayoral Accountability Assembly, 9 April 2008

'It not only helps to knit the loyalty of your staff and thereby to save on your employment costs, it is, of course, the compassionate thing to do.'

Boris Johnson, Mayor, speaking at the Barbican Assembly, 25 November 2009

About 200 people milled around a 167-metre crack in the floor of the Turbine Hall at the Tate Modern gallery on London's south bank. To an onlooker, they appeared to be admiring the daring art installation which was meant to stand for the divisions in the world caused by colonialism and racism.

In fact, they were London Citizens leaders who had gathered to sing Christmas carols.

Just after 5.30 p.m. on 14 December, a powerful lone voice began to sing 'Once in Royal David's City'. People in the hall and on the balcony moved as one towards the crack in the floor.

Negotiations with the Tate had been going on for 18 months with little progress. It was time for action to highlight the poverty wages paid to the cleaning and catering staff who keep the gallery running yet were paid significantly less than the (then) London Living Wage of £7.20 per hour. Members of South London Citizens churches and schools lined up along either side of the *Shibboleth*, joining hands across the crack to express symbolically the gap between the haves and the have-nots in London. The London Citizens Living Wage Campaign banner was unfurled, and the carols began.

The singers then poured out of the Turbine Hall to join TELCO colleagues who had been staging a lively demonstration outside the gallery. Holding placards and banners, and accompanied by a brass band, South London Citizens sang 'We Wish you a Happy Workforce' and other

'Carols for a Living Wage' specially adapted by South .
lead organiser and liturgical composer, Bernadette Farre\
The spectacle was captured live by BBC London, and w\
on BBC Radio 4, in the *Evening Standard* and in the local p\

> *Cleaners and caterers took over the main hall of the Tate Modern gallery as part of a pay protest.*
>
> *Contract workers at the south London gallery say their wage does not cover the true cost of living in the capital.*
>
> *Led by the South London Citizens group, dozens of protesters linked hands and sang in its turbine hall on Friday.*
>
> *A Tate spokesman said: 'Tate ensures all its contractors must comply with the statutory requirement to provide at least the national minimum wage.'*
>
> *Contract workers at the gallery currently receive the national minimum wage of £5.52 per hour.*
>
> *They want this increased to £7.20 per hour, which is known as the London Living Wage – a wage level suggested by mayor Ken Livingstone to reflect the extra cost of living in the capital.*
>
> *South London Citizens spokesman Michael Faulkner said: 'Everyone recognises that living in London is more expensive than living anywhere else.*
>
> *'We believe that the Tate as a major and very successful employer ought to be recognising their responsibilities to make sure that all their employees are properly remunerated for the work that they do.'*[1]

The publicity had the desired effect. South London Citizens met with Tate management to continue negotiations. From 1 April 2009 the Tate agreed to put their cleaners on the London living wage. It cost them no more than the price of the *Shibboleth*.

A community organising maxim is that actions should be 'inside the experience of the organisation, and outside the experience of your opponent'. By singing carols, South London Citizens members were doing what came naturally to them – but in a very alien environment. This 'conquest of space' is a key means of turning the tables on targets who refuse to listen, discomfiting them.

The purpose of applying such pressure is to gain recognition. Only when you are recognised by a power-holder are you in a position to negotiate. Usually, the only means of securing that recognition is by exercising some kind of power. As Saul Alinsky said, 'No one can negotiate until they have the power to compel negotiation.'

Introducing tension – playing hardball, but with gentle means – is vital to recognition. It tells your opponent that you are serious, and organised; but also that you are people of faith and values. Who can object to Christmas carols?

> *Posing as a diverse range of ordinary art fans, around 100 of us waited for our signal (a lone singer and then lined up each side of the crack to link hands and solemnly sing together a range of Christmas Carols. After these songs, we filed out of the huge entrance doors – still singing – to join the more traditional union picket and brass band outside to continue performing seasonal songs with slightly doctored lyrics, including 'we wish you a merry workforce' (my favourite).*
>
> *The effect of all this was so moving that we drew a large audience of spectators inside the gallery and the action inside was described on air as 'incredibly impressive' by the BBC reporter sent to cover it.*
>
> *For me, the most impressive thing about the event was that a high proportion of the demonstrators were actual, in-the-flesh vicars. This is because this highly radical campaign is being organised largely by faith groups and churches across London, alongside unions and student groups. Convinced by the rightness of their demands on behalf of the workers of London, these organisers are prepared to be more militant than most NGOs and are not afraid to be confrontational in their actions or scared to name and shame offending companies.*
>
> *This radicalism means that they are really getting results, and hopes of eventual success with the Tate are therefore high. London Citizens' work has already led to £10 million a year being paid in higher wages across London, with universities, hospitals and the Olympic Delivery Authority already committed to paying a living wage to their lowest paid employees. The Tate is clearly able to afford to pay all its staff decently, and the board cannot be happy at being shamed in such an eyecatching way at Christmas time by a group that includes so many Christians.[2]*

The London Living Wage (LLW)

One of the key concepts in CST is the principle that wages must satisfy the basic needs of a worker and his or her family. By raising his voice in favour of the just wage as early as 1891, Pope Leo XIII was criticising a dogmatic free-market view, prevalent in his time as in our own, that the level of wages should be left to the laws of supply and demand. Yet where employers have a seemingly unlimited supply of workers needing jobs at almost any price, and believe that maximising profits is the key objective of business, what results is exploitation, and a dog-eat-dog mentality. Because of the way the market separates employers from workers – a business, for example, offers a contract to an agency, which in turn employs workers – employers can be in ignorance of the terms and conditions of those who work there. The 'abstraction' of agencies dehumanises.

This is why, at the bottom of the London labour market, a market wage is not a just wage.

Like most other western countries, in the UK since 1999 there has been a statutory National Minimum Wage (NMW), which is the lowest hourly rate employers may legally pay their employees. But it takes no account of the costs of living in the UK. In London, where the basic cost of living is at least 20 per cent higher than elsewhere in the UK, the minimum wage is grossly inadequate to meet the basic needs of a worker and his or her family. Transport, accommodation and food costs are proportionately even more expensive for the very low paid – cleaners, catering staff and porters. Yet too often agencies, under cost pressures from employers, and benefiting from a large pool of young migrant workers from eastern Europe and elsewhere, have taken the view condemned by Pope Leo XIII, that wages 'are regulated by free consent, and therefore the employer, when he pays what was agreed upon, has done his part and seemingly is not called upon to do anything beyond' (*RN* 43).

Cardinal Manning and the just wage

Henry Edward Manning was the son of an MP and banker. Born in 1808, he was educated at Harrow and Balliol, before taking Anglican holy orders; in 1833 he married a member of the Wilberforce family, who died five years later. (As Archbishop of Westminster, he would always remain loyal to Caroline, keeping a photo of her on his desk. When asked who it was, he would simply say: 'My wife'.) He became a Catholic in 1851, was fast tracked into the priesthood by Cardinal Wiseman the same year, and served as the second Archbishop of Westminster from 1865 until his death in 1892, the year after Pope Leo XIII promulgated Rerum Novarum, the encyclical marked by Manning's influence, and by the Church's response to the tensions caused by industrial capitalism.

An ultramontane who promoted temperance, Manning was among other things a vigorous anti-vivisectionist and a tireless champion of Catholic education for the poor, enrolling more than 20,000 children in the schools he had founded. But he is best remembered as a friend of the workers, for his defence of the rights of labour in the age before legal trade unions. To put profit before human dignity, Manning believed, was to invert the moral order. 'If the hours of labour have no other object but the gain of the employer,' he once said, 'no working man can live a life worthy of a dignified human being.'

His famous lecture on the Dignity and Rights of Labour, given at Leeds in 1877, began boldly: 'I claim for labour all the rights of property.' Among them was the right to organise – through unions – to improve conditions. Manning enunciated the famous principle of Rerum Novarum, that a worker's wage should be sufficient to keep his wife and his children, to provide them with decent housing and a healthy diet, and to educate them. It was what the social Catholic movement in the early twentieth century called a 'family wage', and which the alliance of faith and community organisations, London Citizens, today calls a 'living wage'.

Manning's empathy with the workers was perhaps most clearly illustrated by his involvement in the Great Dock Strike of 1889.

After five tense weeks of stand-off between dockers and employers, the cardinal signed the agreement ending the strike. The (mostly Irish) strikers were at that time among the most exploited and defenceless of the workers; and it was Manning's powerful address to the employers that secured them their hike in pay and conditions. But he won praise for holding the scales in balance and The Times, ordinarily hostile to Manning, said his brokering of the strike had won him 'the primacy of all England'.[3]

London Citizens' London Living Wage (LLW) campaign, launched in 2001, is regarded by its leaders as their 'signature' campaign. It has transformed the industrial relations climate among private contractors and their clients in London. Before the campaign started to claim its victories, large employers washed their hands of employment matters, having contracted out their cleaning and catering. But as a result of a series of high-profile London Citizens actions at banks, hotels, shopping centres and university campuses, actions which have confronted employers with the real-life stories of the low-paid staff employed by contractors and agencies, bosses have begun to take greater responsibility for their staff, whether employed directly or indirectly, and to pay them a living wage which at least reflects the costs of living in London (see Table 1 below).

Companies, local authorities, universities and many other employers in London now pay the LLW, or require their contractors to do so. It helped that Ken Livingstone, the former Mayor of London, backed the idea in 2004, and agreed to London Citizens' request that he set up a Living Wage Unit at City Hall, to research and each year set the level of the LLW. And it helped that Boris Johnson, his successor, has maintained that Unit and has thrown his political weight behind the LLW, ensuring that everyone in the Greater London Authority (GLA) is paid it, and urging every employer in London to do so. Queen Mary, part of the University of London, whose Geography Department has tracked the living wage from its beginning, calculates that more than £20m has been paid to more than 6,000 contract workers as a result of the London Citizens' LLW campaign.[4] The living wage is the single most important means of eradicating poverty in London. But there is much still to do: it is estimated that some 400,000 workers in London are still paid less than the LLW. Despite the efforts of the West London Citizens' hotels action team, for example, not a single central London hotel yet pays it. In early 2009, London Citizens, together with Unite's hotel workers branch, published a report into conditions for workers at the hotels, criticising the dependence of luxury hotels on minimum-wage migrant labour.[5]

Table 1: *Mapping the gap between the National Minimum Wage and the London Living Wage*[6]

Year	NMW*	LLW**	Difference	LLW w/o benefits**
2003	4.5	6.40	1.90	
2004	4.85	6.50	1.65	
2005	5.05	6.70	1.65	8.10
2006	5.35	7.05	1.70	9.00
2007	5.52	7.20	1.68	9.15
2008	5.73	7.45	1.72	9.60
2009	5.80	7.60	1.80	9.85

*set by the Government funded Low Pay Commission
(http://www.lowpay.gov.uk)
** calcuated by the GLA from 2005

The living wage campaign goes back to November 2000, when leaders in TELCO, the East London chapter of London Citizens, met to discuss the experience of an IAF living-wage campaign in the American city of Baltimore. Many of the faith leaders present at that retreat spoke of the difficulty that members of their congregations had in taking part in parish life, because of their need to work two minimum-wage jobs to support their children.

In January 2001 London Citizens approached the public sector union UNISON for help; the union commissioned the Family Budget Unit to research a living-wage rate for London, which was published at the end of that year.

At the TELCO assembly at York Hall, Bethnal Green, it was agreed to approach HSBC, which had recently opened a gleaming new headquarters in Canary Wharf. HSBC ignored the approaches, and in December 2001 TELCO occupied a branch of the bank in Oxford Street to protest at the low pay and poor conditions of cleaners at its Canary Wharf site.

After buying shares in the bank, TELCO leaders interrupted an HSBC shareholders' AGM in May 2002 to ask for a meeting with the bank's chairman, Sir John Bond. He agreed; but at the meeting with London Citizens leaders the following month, Sir John rejected the idea of interfering in the market in order to pay cleaners more. But something happened at that meeting which would help him change his mind. After Sir John had protested that HSBC gave millions each year to charity, the Catholic Bishop of Brentwood, who was part of the London Citizens delegation, told him: 'That is all very well, but what is called for here is not charity but justice.'

London Citizens actions are often marked by such 'turning points' or conversion moments. They often happen after a vivid testimony, when the human dimension of a problem suddenly breaks through.

It happened very dramatically at the bank's next shareholder AGM in May 2003. This time, it generated a lot of media attention, not least because the protest coincided with controversy over the HSBC chairman's £2m pay deal. The *Independent* has the story.

They may work in the same office, but they inhabit worlds in vastly different orbits.

Abdul Durrant, 44, who has five children, earns £5 an hour as a cleaner at HSBC's gleaming new tower in London's Docklands. Sir John Bond, chairman of the bank's board, took home a total of £1.88m in the past 12 months and saw his pension pot increase by £272,000 into the bargain.

But yesterday he was forced to listen to the 'invisible man' who cleans at the bank that made £6.42bn last year. Mr Durrant spoke up at HSBC's annual general meeting in London, telling the 22-strong board, who were all wearing matching HSBC ties: 'I am a bit nervous as I have never been in the company of so many big shots. I don't operate a computer, I operate a mop and a bucket. I am supposed to stay invisible, working overnight. I receive £5 an hour. I do not get a pension and there is only a measly sick pay scheme.

'My children go to school without a proper lunch, they cannot go on school trips – I am unable to provide them with all that they need. I am asking you for a living wage, so that I and my colleagues can have the same dignity as ordinary people.'

Mr Durrant earns £200 a week, that is £10,400 a year, working for the company OCS, which is contracted by the bank to clean its new head office in Canary Wharf.

Sir John issued Mr Durrant with an invitation yesterday to come to his office when his late-night cleaning shift begins. 'I am very often in the office until 9pm and would be happy to talk with you again,' Sir John said.

He told Mr Durrant that he 'was very sympathetic' to his cause but that he was obliged to find the best deal for his company. He added: 'I am under pressure to run this business as competitively as I can for shareholders. I cannot dictate to our contractors what they pay their workers.'

Shareholders gave Mr Durrant a round of rousing applause, with one of them asking how much it would hurt the company's multibillion-pound profits to pay its cleaners an extra £1 an hour.[7]

An important technique in community-organising actions is to target two rivals simultaneously. Now Barclays, too, was approached by a London Citizens team. Having angrily rejected the idea, in February 2004 the bank suddenly agreed to new terms and conditions for contract cleaners, including the LLW, employed at its new HQ in Canary Wharf. Watching their rival's humiliation in the press, they had decided to take the initiative. 'We saw what happened with HSBC and then our own annual meeting,' a Barclays spokesman told the *Daily Telegraph*. 'So we went on the front foot. We consulted with a lot of other parties such as the unions and local MPs besides Telco, with whom we worked very positively. On one level yes, this is very much about good corporate social responsibility.'[8]

Barclays's agreement to the LLW in turn helped to persuade HSBC, who signed up to the LLW later that year.

The banks are now leading advocates of the LLW: Barclays appeared alongside the mayor, Boris Johnson, in summer 2008 to champion its benefits. London Citizens was not mentioned as the source of the idea. Nor, generally, is it admitted by LLW employers that many of them first dismissed the idea as immoral, even illegal, so embedded was the view that the free market in salaries was a machine that, left to itself, would over time enrich everyone. Major companies dislike admitting that they are 'giving into pressure' from a people's organisation; it is much better to claim a good idea as its own or, like Barclays, to take the initiative before more pressure can be applied. Most companies can be shown that the LLW is 'the right thing'. But without pressure, it is hard for a company to begin that process of change. 'Change means movement; movement means friction; friction means heat; heat means controversy and conflict', runs another community-organising maxim. Change comes from tension; living with tension is key to success.

At the May 2004 Mayoral Accountability Assembly in Westminster Central Hall, London Citizens called on all candidates to support the establishment of a Living Wage Unit to publish an annual rate for the capital. Ken Livingstone, the successful candidate, agreed. Barclays was praised publicly at the meeting. In May 2004 OCS Cleaning announced a new package for staff at HSBC Canary Wharf (produced in negotiation with HSBC), including a wage increase of 11 per cent to £6.10 an hour – then the LLW rate – as well as holiday and sick pay. The agreement was made two weeks before the HSBC AGM.

In October 2006, Sir John Bond, by now chairman of Vodafone, was on the podium at TELCO's tenth anniversary assembly. 'I feel very humble,' he told the assembly, as he received a garland from TELCO members to huge applause.

Since then the LLW campaign has just kept growing, as more and more banks, businesses, university campuses and shopping centres have agreed to pay the LLW following well-organised campaigns by London Citizens, receiving Living Wage Employer awards at London Citizens assemblies. But some prove stubborn.

A decent day's pay[9]

It is 7 a.m. on Monday, the morning that London's mayor, Boris Johnson, is to announce this year's London Living Wage rate of £7.45 an hour. Outside McDonald's at Liverpool Street Station an unusual clientele is gathering. Four priests, three nuns, a Dominican friar, a Shia Muslim and some 60 congregants of local parishes, some with children in pushchairs, knock back coffee and bagels, their purple London Citizens placards resting between tables. The atmosphere is jolly but tense: a police van waits over the road. We are about to disrupt a business.

Matthew Bolton, lead organiser of the east London chapter of London Citizens, runs through the purpose of today's 'action': to persuade a local hotel, part of the Hyatt chain, to pay its cleaning staff a Living Wage. The Hyatt Andaz Hotel has ignored London Citizens' request for a meeting after the organisation was alerted to low pay there. Stefan Baskerville, in charge of making sure the media are part of the event, thinks BBC London will turn up but has no idea about ITN or PA – the Press Association. But there is a photographer from a catering magazine.

By 7.30 a.m., the BBC and PA arrive just in time as we move down the street to the Andaz. The police make sure the hotel's customers, who pay from £335 to £640 a night, can freely go in and out, while we make sure they learn – from our flyers – that many waitresses,

> *valets and cleaners at the hotel are paid merely the minimum wage allowed by law, £5.52 an hour. Given the high cost of living in the capital, the rate fails to take people out of poverty.*
>
> *We are not expecting a meeting; we just want an appointment. The London Citizens delegation, which includes a vicar-theologian, has been asked to wait outside, along with the TV cameras and our gentle crowd of banner-holding London Citizens leaders.*
>
> *We call this the 'tension'. You ratchet it up, not because you dislike the managers or the investors but because you need them to wake up and look: at the workers, many of them migrants, whose faces are hidden behind the agency contracts; at the churches and mosques and other community organisations that will end up paying, indirectly, for the consequences of poverty; and at the business benefits of paying a living wage.*
>
> *Through the revolving doors we can see two of the managers rapidly running through their options. Doing nothing isn't one of them. Every minute that rolls by knocks a hole in the Hyatt brand. In a few hours this hotel will be on TV, needing to defend the gulf between, on the one hand, its roaring profits in one of the most lucrative trades in the capital, and, on the other, wages that in London condemn workers to poverty. Hyatt can imagine the question: why are you, a profitable company, not paying the Living Wage backed by the capital's Conservative mayor?*

The new Westfield shopping centre in Shepherds Bush was an important target for West London Citizens. 'It took a long while to get an opportunity to talk to the Westfield Group – we had to make and send them a DVD in order to get an appointment,' recalls Valerie Voak, a parishioner at Our Lady of Dolours Servite church in Chelsea.

> Our concern was that there are some very poor areas around White City, where the complex is located, and we want this development to benefit the local people. Over the past two and a half years, we managed to convince them that they should pay the Living Wage to everyone employed directly by the Westfield Group at the site. There will be an ongoing relationship with Westfield – the first stage, getting the developers to commit to the Living Wage, has now come to an end but there will be a second phase of asking the retailers to do the same. It is good to have set the precedent with the centre itself.[10]

'No permanent enemies, no permanent allies' is a community-organising maxim. The enemy who has refused to recognise you becomes a potential ally once he or she does – and a friend when he or she agrees to the community's demands. At West London Citizens' annual assembly in October 2008 – held in a member mosque – Westfield's corporate affairs director, Simon Holberton, received a Living Wage Employer award from Daniella Fetuga-Joensuu of Chelsea Methodist Church.

The case for a living wage

- **KPMG, a leading accountancy firm**

  Ethical behaviour and a commitment to those beyond the shareholders, our people and communities, relies on strong leadership. Paying the Living Wage, and related employment benefits, to our contract cleaners and caterers is part of that commitment – from the top.

  This isn't just about altruism. Corporate Responsibility contributes to more efficient business … It is possible to behave ethically, and pay the Living Wage, while working to earn a profit. It makes sense as a business strategy since it creates goodwill among customers, employees and the community. Trying to increase profits by being unethical or ignoring such concerns will eventually result in increased cost and zero short-term benefit.

  … A business-led movement for social responsibility is our best chance and we can increase the momentum by encouraging others to pay the Living Wage.[11]

- **Queen Mary, University of London**

  The introduction of the Living Wage (at Queen Mary, University of London) has not been the big drain on resources predicted by its opponents: the in-house cleaning service came in only slightly more expensive than that provided by sub-contractors – including start-up costs. When looked at over a two-year period the expected budget for 2008/9 is almost identical to the expenditure spent on contract cleaners in 2006/7 … It's a stance that makes good business sense: investing in training and offering better pay and conditions improves productivity, standards, staff loyalty, performance and turnover without affecting costs. It's a win–win situation for all concerned.[12]

- **Revd Angus Ritchie, TELCO vicar and LLW campaigner**

  People need to be valued, to know that they and their work have worth – and they'll be better workers as a result. That's why hard-nosed executives can be converted to the Living Wage and still stay in post – because they can claim it as a good business idea. Basically what they're accepting is that the view of the human being in church social teaching is more realistic than a cynical view.[13]

Going undercover

One unanticipated consequence of the West London Citizens' hotels LLW campaign has been the discovery that many agency workers are not just paid less than the LLW but *less than the national minimum wage*.

In July 2009, WLC's Hotels Action Team, led by London Citizens organiser Marzena Cichon, enabled BBC2's *Newsnight* team to carry out an undercover report into sharp practices by an agency contracted by the Park Plaza Hotel in Westminster. A Polish journalist and friend to WLC, Ella Sobolewska took a job at Hotelcare, working for £200 a week in conditions she found gruelling and inhuman. With a BBC camera in her shirt button, she recorded hours of interviews with workers and with the agency managers, exposing the ways the agency circumvented minimum-wage legislation by paying per room. It led to a long exposé by the programme. The BBC reported:

> Examination of the time sheets and pay slips of 12 room attendants working for a contract cleaning company at hotels in the Park Plaza chain reveal that they have regularly been paid below the £5.73 per hour minimum adult wage. And two undercover reporters, whom the BBC sent to work as room attendants at the Park Plaza County Hall Hotel and Park Plaza Riverbank, were only paid for about half the number of hours that they actually worked … The agency pays the room attendants not according to the hours they work, but the number of rooms they clean within the working day.[14]

Both the hotel and the agency concerned, Hotelcare, have promised to investigate the abuses and correct them. Two of the managers responsible have been sacked. The workers have been promised their back-pay. West London Citizens is monitoring the progress, keeping up the pressure.

> ### The 400,000 Londoners who earn less than the LLW
>
> *Many workers in London earn well below the living wage rate. The Greater London Authority (GLA) puts the figure at about 1 in 5 or 400,000 people. These workers are clearly not earning the money they should. Many will have dependants to support and they may not have the luxury of other working adults in the family.*
>
> *Our recent research has also found that the majority of workers doing these jobs are migrants to the UK. Many of them are doing the jobs precisely because they are migrants and don't have access to the benefit system. These workers include international students, new arrivals from central and eastern Europe and irregular migrants who are not eligible to claim the in-work benefits that are available to their colleagues. Even if they were paid the London living wage, which would represent a 40 per cent pay rise from the NMW, these workers would need to almost double their income to make up for the lack of support.*
>
> *As a result, many work long hours, take up second or third jobs and share their accommodation with others. I will never forget interviewing one woman from the Caribbean who cleaned at Canary Wharf from 9 p.m. at night, then cleaned a hospital every morning and then managed to look after some elderly people in the evening before returning to clean. This woman had a Herculean appetite for work, sleeping only at the weekend and always falling asleep on the tube going home. She was my age, with a young son at home, and she actually had a stroke during the previous year. Many other workers we have spoken to are similarly studying during the day and working at night.[15]*

Poverty pumpkins

In October 2008, frustrated by the lack of response from the Department of Children, Schools and Families (DCSF) in Whitehall to its request for a meeting to discuss the DCSF's cleaners' wages, London Citizens held a 'Trick or Treat' action to apply a little pressure.

The stars of the action that day were children, drawn from schools and parishes from across the London Citizens alliance. They dressed in Halloween costumes, and went to three Whitehall departments to ask why a meeting had been refused. They were particularly keen to know why, when the DCSF was committed to ending child poverty, they paid their cleaners less than the living wage – which study after study had shown was the minimum needed to bring up children.

> *What I'm aware of, in my congregation and in my work in the community, is the extent to which people struggle on a wage that is significantly less than the London Living Wage. The inevitable casualties of this are health, education and all the elements of social wellbeing we take for granted: the dignity and wherewithal to care for their children as they would like to, and the chance to be participant citizens. What they desperately need are advocates to persuade employers to move from subsisting to flourishing. As long as life is reduced to a desperate struggle to survive, they cannot do this. That is why I passionately support the London Citizens campaign for a living wage.*
>
> The Revd. Joe Hawes, Vicar of All Saints church, Fulham, and member of West London Citizens

Outside the DSCF, they held up a banner that was aimed at the minister in charge of children, Ed Balls. 'Ed, the ball's in your court', it said. London Citizens actions often use the community-organising technique of 'personalising and polarising' – identifying the person responsible for a decision, to prevent them hiding behind faceless bureaucratic 'process', and publicly challenging them to take responsibility.

But the key community-organising maxim, one that is part of the planning of any citizen action, was perfectly illustrated that day: 'The action is the reaction.'

A nervous press officer at the DCSF drafted a statement which was handed to Bridey Purcell, a 12-year-old who is active in South London Citizens. It said the LLW was 'inflationary, artificial and unnecessary' and irresponsible at a time of a credit crunch.

London Citizens passed the statement to David Hencke of the *Guardian* who took it to City Hall for comment. A spokesman for Boris Johnson told Hencke: 'If the government is serious about tackling the capital's obscene levels of poverty and deprivation, then it would join me in urging all London employers to accept the London living wage as the basic pay rate.' He added: 'London is one of the most expensive cities in the world to live and work and it is not only morally right to pay the living wage but also makes good business sense, contributing to better recruitment and retention of staff, higher productivity and a more loyal workforce with high morale.'[16]

Politicians and charities queued up to deplore the minister's response. The irony of a Labour government department opposing the LLW, and a conservative mayor backing it, was not lost on observers.

A reaction to an action can often backfire on the target, leading to a rapid London Citizens win. The reaction exposes the inconsistency, irrationality or immorality of an institution, which the institution is then anxious to cover up.

It was only a matter of days before Ed Balls said the statement had been put out without his approval. In an email to Hencke, the DCSF said: 'The minister is keen to disassociate himself from comments that were attributed to him recently in regard to the living wage. Comments that living-wage policies were unnecessary, artificial and inflationary appear to have been drafted by officials in the department without ministerial clearance.'[17]

Balls had little choice now. He agreed that from 1 April 2009 all staff at his department would be paid the LLW.

That day, more than 1,500 children at schools in membership of London Citizens gathered at the O2 arena for the first ever London Citizens 'Schools Alliance' Assembly. Among the business that day was the presentation of the Living Wage Employer award to the children's minister, Jim Knight.

In October 2009, another 'Trick or Treat' action was held – to persuade two other government departments to pay the LLW. This time the children carried a 'poverty pumpkin' to give to the departments. The Treasury shut its doors, but the Department of Work and Pensions accepted the pumpkin, and agreed to a meeting. On its way back to Methodist Central Hall, the children stopped by the DCSF to award them a golden broom. The people recognised that DCSF had done the right thing, and was now an ally. Pressure, threats, rewards – the techniques Alinsky learned from Chicago street gangs – are turned to good ends on the modern streets of London.

The Parable of the Living Wage: Jack Mahoney SJ on Matthew 20:1–16

All the men in the market place were looking for employment, being in the most insecure social position of daily casual labourers, totally dependent on the law of supply and demand. Yet they had basic needs which had to be satisfied and they had to make a regular living through their work in order to meet their own needs and possibly those of their families.

This recognition of human needs being met through labour was the approach taken by Pope Leo XIII at the end of the nineteenth century, when he pointed out in the midst of the laissez-faire industrial revolution the way in which workers were being disregarded and victimised by being underpaid. As he wrote in the first Catholic social encyclical, Rerum Novarum: *'if one man hires out to another his strength or skill, he does so for the purpose of receiving in return what is necessary for the satisfaction of his needs' (n. 5).*

In the parable of the labourers in the vineyard, we are informed that the wage agreed on with the early morning workers was one denarius (Mt 20:2), which is generally recognised as having been a daily living wage for the time.

Accordingly, when the landowner at the end of the day paid a denarius to all his workers, regardless of how much of the day each had spent in his service, we can think of him as not being simply a generous, or overgenerous, employer, but in fact as being a just employer, in the sense of being one who recognised the need that all his workers had for this amount of payment for their and their dependents' daily sustenance, regardless of the hour at which they joined his work force.[18]

Focus on *Rerum Novarum* (1891)

- *Rerum Novarum* emerged out of many years of discussions of social issues by a variety of Catholics, clergy and laity, and the organisations they founded. *Rerum Novarum* crystallises these ideas, and initiated Catholic social teaching – essentially, a Catholic commentary on modern capitalist society.
- *Rerum Novarum* defended the right of private property (under attack by socialists), argued for a just wage for workers (rather than the contract they were not in a position to refuse), and made clear the right of workers to organise and strike. There was therefore something in it to offend everyone, and each of the groups of the time

(capitalists, revolutionaries, liberals) thought it conceded too much to the other. But it was taken up by thousands of workers who had not been captured by socialism, and 'study circles' organised by worker-swere formed across Europe.

- *Rerum Novarum* was released against the background of revolutionary changes in both politics and the economy. The Industrial Revolution – based on conditions favourable to capital: a steady supply of surplus labour, wages set at the lowest levels possible, long hours of labour – was well advanced, and its consequences were everywhere in displaced and separated families, child labour, poor wages, inadequate housing and dangerous working conditions. These rapid social changes were producing revolutionary politics: the prevailing political orthodoxy of liberalism was challenged by collectivist ideologies of both Left and Right.

- *Rerum Novarum* reflects the thinking of Catholic social reformers who spoke out against the treatment of labour as a commodity, among them Cardinal Manning in England and Frederic Ozanam, founder of the Society of St Vincent de Paul in France. The Fribourg Union offered a critique of both capitalism and socialism and proposed a social theory grounded in Thomist philosophy. The principal author of *Rerum Novarum* was Matteo Liberatore, a neo-Thomist and Jesuit.

Key points

1 At the heart of the encyclical is an insistence on private property as the key element in the resolution of the 'social question'. Leo argues that the reason people work is to obtain property, and that a worker should have the ability to save and dispose of property. (This is a central difference with socialism, which looked to the transfer of property to the state, which would then distribute it.) But while Leo favoured property, he opposed its unlimited expansion. Key to reconciling the right to property with the duty of social obligation is stewardship, which imposes practical obligations which can be imposed by the state if the owners are negligent.

2 Class divisions and inequality are natural, but less important than the equality of all before God. The different classes need each other and are called to cooperate, not be opposed, like different parts of the same body. Each has duties to the other, and by fulfilling these obligations strife will cease.

3   But the Church has a particular concern for the poor. The state is called firstly to rule for the common good, but critically also to protect those who need it most. Poverty is not mostly a sign of moral failure or laziness, but the by-product of an economic system which treats human beings as commodities. The Church and its charitable organisations were insufficient to deal with the problem: the State must play a role through its laws and regulations. Leo cites various elements necessary for resolution the social question: state regulation, just wage, and the organisation of labour.

4   Human beings are not commodities, not merely factors in production like raw materials or capital. People are more than instruments for making money. *Rerum Novarum* attacks the prevailing model of using consent to set wages. In this theory the just wage was what the worker agreed to, and the only injustice was in the worker not performing the agreed work or the employer not paying him or her what was agreed. For Leo, this approach left out a number of vital considerations. Because workers were forced to sell their labour or starve, they cannot be at the mercy of the employer: the price fixed by an employer who can choose whom to employ and a worker who is hungry cannot be compared to a negotiation over the price for a thing, or for labour which is a means of making a profit above what is necessary to survive.

5   The basic principle is that 'a workman ought to have leisure and rest in proportion to the wear and tear of his strength; for the waste of work must be repaired by the cessation of work' (*RN* 33). Women and child labour should be unnecessary; a man's wage should be sufficient to cover their needs – hence the *just wage*.

The popes on the just wage

The just wage is one of the most consistent ideas in Catholic social teaching.

Rerum Novarum (1891)

●   '(T)he employer must never tax his work-people above their strength, not employ them in work unsuited to their sex or age … His great and principal obligation is to give to every one that which is just. Doubtless before we can decide whether wages are adequate many things have to be considered; but rich men and masters should remember this – that to exercise pressure for the sake of gain, upon the indigent and destitute, and to make one's profit out of the need of another, is condemned by all laws, human and divine' (*RN* 16, 17).

- No wage should ever fall below the level to support a worker 'in reasonable and frugal comfort' and 'if through necessity or fear of a worse evil, the workman accepts harder conditions because an employer or contractor will give him no better, he is the victim of force and injustice' (*RN* 34).

- 'Let the working man and the employer make free agreements, and in particular let them agree freely as to the wages; nevertheless, there underlies a dictate of natural justice more imperious and ancient than any bargain between man and man, namely, that wages ought not to be insufficient to support a frugal and well-behaved wage-earner. If through necessity or fear of a worse evil the workman accept harder conditions because an employer or contractor will afford him no better, he is made the victim of force and injustice' (*RN* 45).

Quadragesimo Anno (1931)

- 'In the first place, the wage paid to the workingman should be sufficient for the support of himself and his family ... Every effort must therefore be made that fathers of families receive a sufficient wage adequate to meet ordinary domestic needs. If in the present state of society this is not always feasible, social justice demands that reforms be introduced without delay which will guarantee every adult workingman just such a wage' (*QA* 71).

- Pius XI expanded Leo XIII's teaching in three ways. He added a concern for the state of business and its owners, expressing a firm's capacity for survival as a factor to consider in the setting of wages. Second, if the market is unable to pay a worker a sufficient wage, then social provisions and labour legislation should be introduced to guarantee such a wage. Third, just wages have to be in accord with the requirements of the common good, that is, with the public economic welfare in mind. Wages should be determined in such a way as to offer the greatest number of opportunities of employment and of securing for workers a means of livelihood. 'All are aware that a scale of wages too low, not less than a scale excessively high, causes unemployment' (*QA* 74).

Mater et Magistra (1961)

- 'Our heart is filled with profound sadness when we observe, as it were, with our own eyes a wretched spectacle indeed – great masses of workers who, in not a few nations, and even in whole continents, receive too small a return from their labour. Hence they and their families must live in conditions completely out of accord with human dignity ... Wherefore we judge it to be our duty to reaffirm once again that just as remuneration for work cannot be left entirely to unregulated competition, neither may it be decided arbitrarily at the will of the more powerful . Rather, in this matter, the norms of justice and equity must be strictly observed. This requires that workers receive a wage sufficient to lead a life worthy of man and to fulfil family responsibilities properly' (MM 68, 71).

Laborem Exercens (1981)

- 'In the context of the present there is no more important way for securing a just relationship between the worker and the employer than that constituted by remuneration for work ...'
- 'Just remuneration for the work of an adult who is responsible for a family means remuneration which will suffice for establishing and properly maintaining a family and for providing security for its future. Such remuneration can be given either through what is called a family wage – that is, a single salary, given to the head of the family for his work, sufficient for the needs of a family without the other spouse having to take up gainful employment outside the home – or through other social measures such as family allowances or grants to mothers devoting themselves exclusively to their families' (LE 19).

Centesimus Annus (1991]

- 'Alienation is found also in work, when it is organised so as to ensure maximum returns and profits with no concern whether the worker, through his own labour, grows or diminishes as a person, either through increased sharing in a genuinely supportive community or through increased isolation in a maze of relationships marked by destructive competitiveness and estrangement, in which he is considered only a means and not an end' (CA 41).

Focus on *Laborem Exercens*

- Published in 1981, to celebrate the ninetieth anniversary of *Rerum Novarum*, *Laborem Exercens* was written largely by Pope John Paul II himself, who revised the document while recovering in hospital after a gunman's attempt on his life. The Pope puts forward positive view of work as sharing in the activity of the Creator. He issued the encyclical at a time of an all-pervasive materialism and consumerism and an all-consuming drive for efficiency and profit.

- *Laborem Exercens* is the most comprehensive treatment of human work in CST. It goes beyond *Rerum Novarum*'s focus on manual labour to include other kinds of work.
- *Laborem Exercens* centres on two key concepts: work is for the person, not the person for the work. And labour has priority over capital.

Key points

1 The source of the dignity of work is to be found in the fact that it is done by people, rather than in the work that is done. In other words, work has an ethical value of its own, linked to the worker as a person, who is free and self-determining. Work is the way in which people exercise the distinctive human capacity for self-expression and self-realisation. Work also has a strong social dimension – it is for the family, and for society as a whole. Thus if the division and organisation of work become unjust, it is the family and the nation which are harmed.

2 The error of 'economism' arises when labour is valued only in terms of its economic purpose; this is the mistake of materialism, which sees work only as production and consumption. Thus apparently 'economically unproductive' work – raising children, or working in the voluntary sector – tends to be devalued, and workers are regarded as instruments rather than ends (exploitation). The symptoms of the latter are inadequate wages or oppressive working conditions, and when personal satisfaction and incentives to creativity and responsibility are lacking (*LE* 5). Labour can be alienating, when men and women are denied participation in the enterprise.

3 Both the ideology of capitalism (liberalism) and socialism (Marxism) are guilty of separating capital from labour, in the sense that the person is subordinated to either profit or class (*LE* 11). By capital Pope John Paul II means machines and natural resources (including money) which the capitalists own, as well as 'the small but highly influential group of entrepreneurs, owners or holders of the means of production' (*LE* 11). By labour he means ordinary workers who lack the means of production and who share in the process of production by virtue of selling their labour.

4   Unlike Marxism, the moral legitimacy of private ownership is accepted, but unlike liberal capitalism, this is not seen as an absolute right. The 'invisible hand' of the market is not to be trusted to harmonise conflicting interests, nor will the free market solve the problem of unemployment. There is no intrinsic opposition between capital and labour, which are 'inseparably linked' (*LE* 13); capital is accumulated labour, and the result of human work. Capital and labour should work together for the common good.

5   *Laborem Exercens* provides the strongest support in CST for labour unions and the right of workers to organise. Unions are 'an indispensable element of social life' (*LE* 20). The 'ethical vocation' of unions is not just to secure rights for its members within the constraints of the common good, but also to promote solidarity and social justice. But John Paul II warns that while unions need to enter the political sphere to accomplish their objectives, they should not become political parties or have too close links to them (*LE* 20).

6 DWELLING IN DIGNITY

The principle of the universal destination of goods requires that the poor, the marginalised and in all cases those whose living conditions interfere with their proper growth should be the focus of particular concern.

Compendium of the Social Doctrine of the Church (182)

While I was speaking to the two children (6, 3) they were sitting in the empty bathtub as there was literally no floorspace.

South London Citizens, 'Housing Our Future' report

If you were crossing Tower Bridge at 8 a.m. on 30 July 2007, you would have marvelled at the sun in a clear sky glinting off the River Thames. But what would have surprised you even more was a row of bright red tents along the south bank of the river, right next to City Hall.

'Tent City', London Citizens called it, although, as it happens, the tents were only erected for a day because the action produced the necessary result. The tent action was part of a campaign that started in 2004 calling for those at the bottom of the income ladder – the ones whom London Citizens have argued should be paid at least the living wage – to be able over time to own their own homes.

'Our Homes, Our London' starts from recognising a situation well known to any young married couple or average-earning person in London: the virtual impossibility of buying a flat or house, and being condemned to rent at ever higher rates which rise in line with property prices. It is a campaign with a workable, realistic, practical solution which London Citizens has succeeded in persuading the capital's mayor to adopt, one which holds out the future prospect of challenging the housing market in the way that the LLW campaign has challenged the wage market.

In the US, housing has been one of the key areas of community organising. One of the best known is the Nehemiah Homes project in New York, which takes its name from the Old Testament prophecy in the book of Nehemiah to rebuild the walls of Jerusalem. Since IAF-East created and implemented the nation's first Nehemiah housing effort in 1982 in Brooklyn, IAF affiliate East Brooklyn Congregations has built 2,900 new townhouses in formerly blighted areas, with another 840 homes now in the pre-development stage.

> An organisation with a core budget of three hundred thousand dollars a year, a staff of four, and a modest headquarters in a local apartment complex halted two decades of burning, deterioration and abandonment by building a critical mass of owner-occupied town houses and generating a chain reaction of other neighbourhood improvements. EBC built on every large parcel and abandoned block in the area – 140 acres. The market value of the housing built now exceeds $400 million.

> The group succeeded in large part because its leaders creatively applied the lessons absorbed during the sponsoring committee phase to the challenge of rebuilding a wasteland with homes affordable to working families making as little as $25,000 a year. Instead of beginning by asking government for funding, the leaders of EBC first raised $8 million of no-interest revolving construction funding from their own church bodies – the Roman Catholic Diocese of Brooklyn, the Episcopal Diocese of Long Island, and the Lutheran Church Missouri Synod.[1]

In Chicago, United Power, an IAF affiliate with 330 dues-paying members, has created a similar initiative, known as Ezra Community Homes:

> Drawing on the social knowledge developed by the IAF over the past twenty-five years, beginning with the Nehemiah homes in New York, United Power's goal is to build thousands of affordable homes for low- and moderate-income working families over a ten-year period. The organization secured $5.2 million in interest-free loans to fund home construction, won passage of a Chicago city council ordinance to authorize property transfers for 140 sites in a devastated Westside area of the city, conducted homeowner education sessions with more than 300 interested individuals, prescreened the first prospective Ezra buyer families, qualified the first group for Ezra financing and subsidies, and secured a signed contract from the city's Commission on Housing, which authorized groundbreaking on 140 sites in North Lawndale for construction of the first Ezra homes for working families.[2]

A ladder out of reach

London's sharply escalating property prices have led to a growing divide between the haves and the have-nots. For the have-nots, the closest they get to the ladder is the sight of the bottom rung far above their heads.

If you're on the property-owning ladder, you have the chance to make substantial profits by buying and selling; even if you don't speculate with your property, you are protected from housing inflation by the fact that your own house is rising in value along with the market, giving you access to cheap loans through mortgages.

But if you cannot get on the ladder because you earn the salary of a teacher, nurse or construction worker, or do not have a lump of capital to put down as a deposit, you have to watch while the lowest rung of that ladder keeps rising far faster than your salary. And because rents rise along with property prices, your rent will keep increasing, eating up an ever larger proportion of your salary. You are condemned, in other words, to be excluded from the mechanisms of exchange, while the people that own properties – especially more than one property – cannot fail, as long as the market keeps rising, to get richer, or at least to remain level.

> *It is in fact the weakest who are the victims of dehumanising living conditions, degrading for conscience and harmful for the family institution. The promiscuity of working people's housing makes a minimum of intimacy impossible; young couples waiting in vain for a decent dwelling at a price they can afford are demoralised, and their union can thereby even be endangered; youth escape from a home which is too confined and seek in the street compensations and companionships which cannot be supervised. It is the grave duty of those responsible to strive to control this process and to give it direction. (OA 11)*

This is a bad thing for any society. It makes for insecurity, and hopelessness. It discourages people from getting married and having children. It means that at the bottom end of society – although not necessarily the very poor, who have at least the *right* to social housing, if not access in practice – people have no investment in their surroundings. The fabric of society is consequently weakened.

The statistics tell their own story. Salaries in London have increased in London by 26 per cent since 1997, while house prices and rents have increased by a staggering 127 per cent. The average cost of a house in

London is £350,000, and the average deposit for a first-time buyer £51,000. People earning £25,000 cannot hope to own their own homes unless they move into a considerably higher earning bracket. Some 175,000 families live in overcrowded accommodation ('severe' over-crowding in London increased by 60 per cent between 1991 and 2001), with more than 260,000 children in London living in homes without enough bedrooms. Some 30 per cent of people leaving London cited housing as their main reason for leaving. And 72 per cent of businesses cite lack of affordable housing as the main obstacle to recruiting staff.[3]

Those worst affected by soaring house prices are not the very poor but those on low to average incomes, who are forced to pay escalating rents for often inadequate housing. Some 55 per cent of newly built homes are sold not to working families but to buy-to-let investors.

At London Citizens assemblies and meetings, this was continually mentioned as a key concern: being unable to hope to own property was time and time again identified as one of the big factors undermining the fabric of the community. Home ownership is an expression of human dignity. It is good for people and good for society. It gives people security and a stake in the community.

The result was the 'Our Homes, Our London' campaign for affordable housing through Community Land Trusts (CLTs). One of its key aims was to ensure that some of the land used on the site of London Olympics 2012 be given over to a CLT. In May 2007, London Citizens established the East London Citizens Community Land Trust as an Industrial/Provident Society regulated by the Financial Services Authority. London Citizens is now campaigning to establish the capital's first Community Land Trust, to offer an attractive example of what the campaign calls 'community-owned, community-orientated, perpetually affordable housing across the capital'.[4]

CST and the right to a decent home

CST attaches enormous importance to dignified housing, seeing it as vital to the well-being of family. Article 11 of the Church's 'Charter of the Rights of the Family' reads: 'The family has the right to decent housing, fitting for family life and commensurate to the number of the members, in a physical environment that provides the basic services for the life of the family and the community.'⁵ The Vatican's Justice and Peace Council in 1987 noted how the lack of housing acted as a deterrence to families and young children:

> Often enough, the amount of money needed to acquire a decent home, coupled with a housing shortage, involves long and painful delays before they can find a place to live. This situation sometimes creates serious obstacles to their right to found a family. Such concrete difficulties often constitute a psychological barrier for these young people and are a veritable dissuasive force when it comes to assuming a commitment to marriage. Those who do get married, despite all of these conditioning factors, sometimes have to live with their parents for a long time or struggle with the burden of housing costs or high rents for a number of years. This situation has negative consequences for their life together and on the healthy development of this new family. It is not rare that the first years of married life are conditioned by such exterior factors that result in an almost forced delay in having children. This, in turn, troubles the harmony of conjugal life and is detrimental to both society and the Church.⁶

The same document describes the lack of housing as a 'scandal' and 'one more indication of the unjust distribution of goods, originally destined for the use of all.' And it adds: 'Any person or family that, without any direct fault of his or her own, does not have suitable housing, is the victim of an injustice.'⁷

Pope John Paul II saw the lack of housing in developed as well as underdeveloped countries as a clear sign of problems in the model of economic development:

> The lack of housing is being experienced universally and is due in large measure to the growing phenomenon of urbanization. Even the most highly developed peoples present the sad spectacle of individuals and families literally struggling to survive, without a roof over their heads or with a roof so inadequate as to constitute no roof at all. The lack of housing, an extremely serious problem in itself, should be seen as a sign and summing-up of a whole series of shortcomings: economic, social, cultural or simply human in nature. Given the extent of the problem we should need little convincing of how far we are from an authentic development of peoples. (*SRS* 17)

CST lists housing as an 'essential service' connected to the integrity and promotion of a person and his or her fundamental rights. In other words, it constitutes a basic social good on which the common good depends. (The others are: food, work, education and access to culture, transportation, basic health care, freedom of communication and expression, and the protection of religious freedom (*CSDC* 166)). As with the just wage, therefore, housing cannot be simply to the market alone; nor should housing be considered solely or mainly a market commodity. Both the lack of housing and the inadequacy of housing (overcrowding and insecurity) are listed in CST as one of 'the miseries of today's world' and efforts to tackle them as a means of defending the dignity of the human person (*CSDC* 535). Access to housing and home ownership, the rights of tenants and owners, overcrowding and affordability – these are issues to which solutions need to be found, in the interests both of justice and of the common good, and especially because of the effect of lack of housing on the poor:

> The Church is very conscious that the lack of decent housing threatens the dignity and rights of the poorest. That is why one of the fundamental criterion for judging the justice or injustice of political and economic decisions is their effective repercussions on those on the fringes of society. Indeed, the fact of effectively dealing with different situations of poverty is a true test of the way that those with societal responsibilities are fulfilling their duty of justice.[8]

The Vatican has called for a consistent political will to be developed to tackle this question, noting that 'a just housing policy must necessarily include the participation of the private sector as well as that of the State'. It emphasised the need for civil-society institutions, including the Church, to seek solutions:

> Mention has already been made several times of the necessity of assuring the broadest possible participation of the different sectors of society in the development of housing policies. Experience has shown that, along side of public authorities, and sometimes even before them, certain private and public organizations are working to remedy the lack of housing and to help homeless individuals or families. The action of the Church finds its place within this context.

An important point to be emphasized is that the problem of the lack of decent housing concerns not only the millions of peoples who are its victims, nor even institutions, but is also a challenge to every man and woman with a house and who discovers or becomes more keenly aware of the extent and depth of the drama of those without one. Each one of us should feel obliged to do what he or she can do, either directly or indirectly, through various existing organizations, so that others can also enjoy a right of which they have been deprived.[9]

CST's view of housing is not just concerned with the dignity of the dwelling, but also with the question of ownership. The popes have consistently urged that people be able to come to own the place they live in over time. Leo XIII said that the law 'should favour ownership, and its policy should be to induce as many people as possible to become owners', essentially through just wages, which allow a worker to save towards the cost of his or her home (*RN* 35). 'The Church's social doctrine', notes the *Compendium*, 'requires that ownership of goods be equally accessible to all, so that all may become, at least in some measure, owners' (*CSDC* 176).

> *Here, again, we have further proof that private ownership is in accordance with the law of nature. Truly, that which is required for the preservation of life, and for life's well-being, is produced in great abundance from the soil, but not until man has brought it into cultivation and expended upon it his solicitude and skill. Now, when man thus turns the activity of his mind and the strength of his body toward procuring the fruits of nature, by such act he makes his own that portion of nature's field which he cultivates – that portion on which he leaves, as it were, the impress of his personality; and it cannot but be just that he should possess that portion as his very own, and have a right to hold it without any one being justified in violating that right. (RN 9)*

CST repeatedly links land ownership to the concept of stewardship: property ownership carries obligations. Land is a God-given resource, which we administer: 'Land shall not be sold in perpetuity, for the land belongs to me, and to me you are only strangers and guests' (Leviticus 25:23).

CST distinguishes between land and capital. Land is God-given, whereas capital is the fruit of human labour. A house or block of flats –

buildings standing on plots of land – requires both. The Church affirms the natural right to ownership of capital precisely because it is a product of human effort, and people have a natural right to the full fruits of their labour. But if land is God-given, and not the product of anyone's labour, then there can be no natural, *absolute* right of ownership. That is why CST calls for land to be fairly distributed, and why the Church has consistently defended common land.

Private property on common land

In the eighteenth century Thomas Spence and later the Chartists argued – as does CST – that property ownership was a necessary precondition for freedom and dignity of families, and that land should be held in common. They were reacting against the trend of that century in which the vast majority of land came to be owned by a small class of landowners, who would lease out the land at high prices.

The Chartists' campaign for land held in common – known as 'community land trusts' – were the inspiration behind an idea adopted by Martin Luther King and which has become popular in the United States. When a community owns the land that properties are built on – not the properties themselves, but the land – the price is taken out of the property price, reducing it by around 60 per cent.

After studying various models, London Citizens put forward a plan combining a Community Land Trust (CLT) with a Mutual Home Ownership Trust (MHOT). The idea is to exclude permanently the cost of land from the cost of homes, enabling low- and average-income workers to buy their own homes while preserving the affordability of those homes for the next generation. The homes are affordable, and stay affordable; but they are still sold for a profit, enabling workers to move up the housing ladder as their circumstances improve. [10]

It works like this. Land is 'granted' – released by a local authority, say – to a CLT at no cost, and the Trust safeguards it in democratic public ownership. Next an MHOT is set up, which leases the land from the Trust. The MHOT raises the finance to build the homes, and subsequently lets the homes to members of the MHOT – who would normally be people in the neighbourhood. Residents' payments cover the costs of the mortgages (about 30–35 per cent of salary) as well as costs of management, maintenance and cleaning. If they leave, residents take with their initial deposit as well as their share of the equity, including 90 per cent of the increase in its value. That means that the buyer gets to buy that property at only a slightly higher price than the previous owner, while the seller gets to keep most of the profit.

Unlike other shared-ownership models, permanent affordability is guaranteed for generation after generation of low- to average-income earners. The CLT brings security and dignity and a stake in the community. The crucial decisions about the running of the properties are made by the residents themselves, together with other residents.

Camping on the river

Armed with the information and the model, London Citizens approached the then mayor, Ken Livingstone. At a TELCO assembly in 2004 he agreed to study the scheme. Over the next three years London Citizens kept up the pressure until a site was found for a pilot scheme in Bow, East London. But by 2007 there had still been no concrete commitment. It was time to bring pressure. Citizen organising is not just about persuading powerful people to agree; it is also about pressuring them into the action which follows agreement.

Frustrated at the lack of progress, London Citizens organised a 'Tent City' action on Potter's Field outside City Hall.

Potter's Field is a stretch of parkland administered by Southwark Borough Council that runs between City Hall – the seat of the mayor – and Tower Bridge. We set up the rows of bright red tents at 6 a.m. that morning. The plan had been kept under wraps, to increase impact and prevent last-minute injunctions. We put out a press release, organised materials to hand out, and gathered: Buddhists, Muslims from East London's mosque and dozens of Catholic and other Christian parishioners with their priests and pastors gathered, chatted and prayed. The Parks Authority soon turned up and asked people to leave. We explained what we were doing and why we were doing it. We asked about the laws which prevented us from being there. The Authority staff, unsure, went off to consult.

They came back and told us we were in violation of various bye-laws which included engaging in 'political and religious activities' on Potter's Field. But they agreed to let us stay to celebrate Mass as long as we dismantled the tents. They seemed much less angry now. It was hard to feel threatened by a group of Buddhists praying in a circle outside a tent on a sun-struck day in July.

The matter was put to a vote, and we agreed. By that time, a photo of our tent city had appeared on the front page of the *Evening Standard*, and BBC London had sent TV crews to follow events. We had won public attention. The 'action is in the reaction'. We thanked the Southwark officials for their patience and indulgence. We had achieved our objectives.

Fr Tom O'Brien, an Assumptionist priest at Bethnal Green whose parish is a member of TELCO, celebrated an open-air Mass opposite the Tower of London. The Revd Angus Ritchie, an East End priest and Anglican theologian of community organising, preached the homily.

Just then Neale Coleman, the mayor's chief housing policy officer, came out of City Hall to tell campaigners and TV cameras that he was confident the scheme would work and could be 'rolled out across London' in future years. The challenge, he added, was to persuade major landowners in London – local authorities, the NHS and the Ministry of Defence – to hand over land to the trusts. But he assured us that he was committed to the pilot programme going ahead, and even supplied dates and a timetable.

Coleman told us he was glad we were putting on pressure. It helps politicians who are committed to a path of action to be seen to be responding to popular demands. London Citizens actions are designed to put a squeeze on recalcitrant or obtuse targets, but able politicians and public officials can turn it to their advantage.

The next day Ken Livingstone posed for photographs alongside campaigners with 'Our Homes, Our London' placards, and at the start of his press conference drew journalists' attention both to the campaign and to the pilot scheme in Bow.

It turned out that, for legal reasons, the land in Bow was unavailable. In the meantime, Boris Johnson was elected mayor. At the London Citizens Mayoral Accountability Assembly in April 2008 he declared himself in support of the CLT idea, and to work with London Citizens.

In October 2008 members of the housing team voted to persuade City Hall to look at giving over public land at the St Clements hospital site in Mile End as a CLT. Meanwhile, London Citizens has persuaded the Olympic Development Authority actively to pursue the possibility of part of the Olympics 2012 land in Stratford to be given over as a CLT.

As a result of our action – strategic, peaceful, determined – London Citizens has won for Londoners the possibility of a future in which housing becomes affordable for low-paid workers, to the benefit not just of those who will have their own homes, but the society around us.

Affordable homes for workers and their families is the answer not just to the housing crisis but is also part of the answer to the breakdown of civic and community life in the capital.

Housing Affordability Standard (HAS)

What does 'affordable housing' actually mean? The term is often deployed in housing contracts, when Government or a Council stipulates that a certain number of private housing units be 'affordable'. But there is no agreed standard, and in practice it means any housing that is made available at less than full market value. It does not mean affordable by those on LLW, let alone the minimum wage.

A definition was provided by Zacchaeus 2000 Trust in May 2005: 'Affordable housing means that once the cost of rent or mortgage (including any maintenance and service charges) and local and national taxes have been met from the income of a household, be it an individual, a family, or pensioners, there remains sufficient income to sustain safe and healthy living, to support children's needs at school and to enable provision for the future and participation in the community. "Unaffordable" housing means that the remaining income is not sufficient to ensure these outcomes.'[11]

This standard was calibrated in 2008 using the Minimum Income Standards (MIS) methodology developed by York University – the same methodology that was used to calculate the LLW. London Citizens asked Professor Peter Ambrose, Professor in Housing Studies at the University of Brighton, to calculate a definition of affordable housing that can be applied in East London across three household types (2 adults + 2 children, 1 adult + 2 children, and a person living alone), assuming that the earner in each household is paid the LLW.

At the Mayoral Accountability Assembly at Methodist Central Hall in April 2008, Boris Johnson agreed to use this methodology in order to calculate and publish an HAS figure annually, as City Hall does with the LLW.

One of the aims of Our Homes, Our London is to promote the incorporation of the HAS into private housing building contracts, to ensure that in future housing really does become affordable – for those who most need it to be.[12]

A Christmas message from the children of St Mary's Battersea

If the Community Land Trust scheme holds out the future prospect of low-paid Londoners having access to private property, the urgent problem of chronic overcrowding remains. The space available for large families in London has shrunk since the early 1980s, when three- or four-bedroom council houses were sold to owner-occupiers without the need of such space. The result is a severe shortage of housing for large families in London.

When Michael Lobo was appointed headteacher of St Mary's Roman Catholic primary school in Battersea, South London, he was keen to raise its profile and deepen its links to the local community. The school was a member of South London Citizens (SLC), and its local chaplain, Fr John Clark, was a great supporter. Mr Lobo invited SLC's Dermot Bryers to give English classes to the parents in the school, many of whom were immigrants. After one of the classes, a Kosovan woman, Hadjie Rizana, told Dermot that she lived with her husband and three children in a one-bedroom flat, and the Council was unable to rehouse them. Could he help her?

The matter was taken to the SLC Strategy Meeting, where representatives of the member institutions agree on campaigns and actions. They agreed to do some 'action research' to find out how widespread was the problem of overcrowding at the school. It soon became clear, from parents' meetings, that there were countless stories of families of five or more squeezed into one-bedroom flats. One mother was living in one room with her husband and two young children. 'It was a real shock,' says Lobo. 'The children were coming to school clean and well dressed. We had absolutely no idea they were living in such conditions.'[13]

A meeting was arranged with the director of housing at Wandsworth Council, at which Hadjie spoke powerfully about the impact on her children of so many in such a confined space. There was a long silence after she spoke. Fr John asked: 'Mr Evans, would you say this was an isolated experience?' Evans answered: 'Sadly, no.' The SLC team said they wanted to conduct a survey to see if the experience was repeated in the local area. He raised no objection.

With Lobo's support, SLC surveyed 100 parents registered in Wandsworth who had children at St Mary's. Of the 62 surveys returned, 52 per cent were overcrowded by national criteria, and 81 per cent by Wandsworth's own more realistic criteria. As well as lack of space to study at home, the effects of overcrowding on children's educational, social and emotional development is obvious and well documented.

South London Citizens invited Evans to its annual assembly to discuss the findings, but he declined. The team decided to send him a DVD Christmas message, which quickly became a hit on YouTube and was covered at length in the *Guardian*. 'A message to Mr Roy Evans, Director of Housing at Wandsworth Council, from the children of St Mary's primary school, Battersea' is a brilliant example of one of community organising's most lethal weapons. It is hard to watch it without shedding a tear: the children cheerfully explain that in spite of being 'a bit squashed' they still come to school, and ask Mr Evans if he can 'fix it' for them. 'Can you fix it? Yes you can!' they cry. 'My best Christmas present ever would be a nice warm, cosy room', says one; 'For Christmas, I'd like a place to do my homework', says another, before the children launch into 'Be near me, Lord Jesus! / I ask Thee to stay / Close by me forever / And love me, I pray'. The children ask Mr Evans for Christmas promises: 'To set up a team of people who will visit some of our homes and see how they can be fixed', 'to ask the people who look after us to help you – a citizens' panel', and 'to make changes in our homes so we are not squashed any more'. The children end with a rousing 'We wish you a merry Christmas'.

'We were trying to show the truth through the eyes of the children,' says Bernadette Farrell. 'If you believe the Scriptures, children see things clearest of all. In terms of human experience and spirituality, they're the leaders. Jesus puts them in front of us and says, "be like this". It was the children speaking the truth that made things happen – and a headteacher with the breadth of vision to trust the children. Their experience is what matters. They know what it's like – and they've got some of the best ideas.'

> There are times when the children come to the school very distressed or falling asleep or just not being able to pay attention in class. We didn't really know what the reasons could be, but it became obvious that their lives at home were affecting their academic performance, and this just wasn't acceptable. The housing survey and the home visits that we did have helped us to understand why the children are coming to school like this, and we're determined to improve things. We need larger homes locally, but in the meantime there are other things we can do, such as making available the school and its recreation areas to parents. Open space is such a vital thing for our children. One of the reasons

> *our school is now so successful is because the children have so much*
> *space to let off steam. We are very proud to be part of South*
> *London Citizens, and we hope that the Council and the*
> *Government will work with us to improve the space of households*
> *in the area.*[14]

Whether they feature children or adults or both, London Citizens' DVDs
– usually addressed to a particular person on the community-organising
principle of 'personalise and polarise' – are direct, human appeals which
cut through the pseudo-objectivity behind which people with power try
to hide. The council housing director's response, as reported by the
Guardian – 'London Citizens has carried out some useful work here, but
this is just one of 50 primary schools in Wandsworth, and we've got
thousands of people on various waiting lists' – is a classic obfuscation.[15]
The DVD punctures this smokescreen by foregrounding the urgent,
human, local need: *these* children in *this* place are living in overcrowded
accommodation. But their teachers and parents are not simply frustrated
and complaining. They are able and willing to help the local authority
find solutions.

South London Citizens went on to conduct two more overcrowding
surveys at primary schools in Wandsworth borough. In Balham (Alder-
brook and Trinity St Mary's), the same pattern was revealed: serious
overcrowding, with damaging effects on children's health and learning.
South London Citizens decided to form a Citizens Housing Commission,
appointing four commissioners to hear more evidence and come up with
workable solutions that could be put into practice by housing associations, the council, the government, as well as by local communities. 'The
idea is that change can happen if we work together,' explains Bernadette
Farrell.

> *My name is Argjenta Rizana, I am 9 years old and I am in class 5*
> *at St Mary's primary school. I live in Battersea with my mum and*
> *dad, my seven-year-old sister and my five-year-old brother. We*
> *have one bedroom, so it's quite squashed and I have to share a*
> *small bedroom with my whole family. It's hard because we go to*
> *bed at different times. Sometimes it's difficult to get to sleep. I like*
> *my family but I'd love to have a bedroom of my own, but I don't*
> *know how long I'll have to wait because the Council said there*
> *aren't any homes with three bedrooms.*[16]

Over the summer of 2009, local SLC leaders carried out dozens of home visits, and met to share ideas about how to improve living conditions in overcrowded homes. They gathered 302 testimonies, including those of 140 children, from 125 households. In September, they invited the council to hear their findings – a meeting attended by 15 council representatives.

In December 2009, SLC published its 'Housing Our Future' report into the effects of overcrowding on children in Wandsworth, concluding that overcrowding was severe and affecting the lives of children and their futures.[17] It identified the lack of three- and four-bedroom homes, and among a raft of other recommendations called urgently for more family-sized houses to be prioritised. The report is unusual in that, despite being written by commissioners with long expertise in housing, and packed with statistics and analysis, it gives the leading voice to the children's own experience, as articulated through words and pictures. The children are the 'alternative experts' of the report – the ones who see the truth because they live with it.

SLC leaders have asked for regular meetings with the council, offering their time and expertise to help it implement the recommendations – 'to fix it so we are not squashed any more'.

Argjenta and her family have now been re-housed.

Focus on *Sollicitudo Rei Socialis*

- Pope John Paul II wrote *Sollicitudo Rei Socialis* in 1987 to celebrate the twentieth anniversary of Pope Paul VI's *Popolorum Progressio*. The encyclical surveys global changes since that landmark docu-ment, changes which were a fruit of increasing globalisation, and offers a strong critique of the model of development which is pro-ducing greater division between the haves and the have-nots.

- John Paul II notes three critical symptoms of underdevelopment: the housing crisis, unemployment and international debt. Neither West-ern liberal capitalism nor the Eastern Communism had proved capa-ble of 'a true and integral development of individuals and peoples in modern society' (*SRS* 21).

- The positive development in modern society was, however, the growth of solidarity and a recognition of the interdependence of all peoples.

- The encyclical is concerned with a true concept of development – not 'having' but 'being' more. The Church must raise its voice, says John Paul II, 'when the 'having' of a few can be to the detriment of the "being" of the many' (*SRS 31*).

- The key virtue here is 'solidarity', a term which the encyclical uses 27 times. Previous popes used terms such as 'friendship' (Leo XIII), 'social charity' (Pius XI) and 'civilisation of love' (Paul VI). For John Paul II, it is a central concept in CST which brings together charity and justice. Solidarity helps us 'to see the "other" … as our "neighbour", a "helper" to be made a sharer, on a par with ourselves' (*SRS* 39); it is not just vague compassion but 'a firm and persevering determination to commit oneself to the common good; that is to say to the good of all and each individual, because we are all really responsible for all' (*SRS* 38). It is variously a principle, an attitude, a value and a virtue.

7   WELCOME, STRANGER

Yesterday thousands of fellow human beings were given what we all prize most – recognition. They were able to assert their right to be more than cheap cogs in a business wheel. The moment was fleeting as they disappeared in the rain. But this new taste will remain and inspire. If enough determined people try to make something happen – then it will. These strangers will become citizens.

Neal Lawson[1]

May Bank Holiday 2009, Parliament Square: a once-in-a-generation eruption, in the public square, of faith – and a powerful call rooted in the constant message of the Bible for the foreigner to be welcomed and assisted.

By the time they had left services in Westminster Cathedral, Westminster Abbey and Methodist Central Hall – the first time in living memory that the nation's three mother churches had joined together in this way – and met up in Parliament Square with Muslims, trade unionists and refugee groups, the crowd numbered about 7,000. At St Margaret's Church, Westminster, a Zimbabwean choir lifted the Revd Ralph Godsall's prayer 'that a pathway into citizenship may be granted to those whose basic human rights have been denied', while over at Westminster Cathedral, where four years before the Strangers into Citizens campaign began at a multilingual Mass, Bishop Thomas McMahon of Brentwood opened with a call to bring people 'out of degradation into dignity, out of darkness into light – from strangers into citizens'. In his homily, Bishop Patrick Lynch, an auxiliary of Southwark who is in charge of the bishops' committee on migration, told a packed congregation of 3,000:

> A migrant's legal status is quite separate from his or her human dignity. A human being's worth is defined by their God-given dignity, not by the papers they do or do not carry. There is a clear moral case that undocumented workers who have lived and worked in this country for five years or more should be given the opportunity to build a future in the United Kingdom and continue to contribute to British society. You have worked here. Your children

have been born here, and attend school here. You are part of our parishes and our society here, and a way should be found so that you can remain here.

Spilling out of the churches, carrying bright orange placards with the words 'STRANGERS INTO CITIZENS: CALL FOR A PATHWAY INTO CITIZENSHIP FOR LONG-TERM MIGRANTS', the supporters mobilised by London Citizens from across the country walked behind a banner held by bishops, imams and rabbis. Once they reached Trafalgar Square, where a stage was set for music and speeches, they formed part of an even larger pool of some 18,000 people. It was the largest ever rally in support of immigrants in British history, a conquest of public space with a message that mixed human rights with social integration. These were immigrants, many of them 'illegal'; yet they carried Union flags, symbols of patriotism and national pride. Their message: we are loyal citizens, who want to be given the chance to be allowed to participate as legal ones.

The radical call of Strangers into Citizens came directly from CST. Appropriately, it had all begun at a celebration of the Eucharist in the UK's mother Catholic church three years before, when the Cardinal Archbishop of Westminster made the first call by a UK religious leader for a pathway into citizenship for immigrants without status. It would lead to a campaign which has placed the spotlight on a large, stable population in Britain living outside the protection of the law, whose plight politicians have tried desperately to avoid confronting.

London Citizens and irregular migrants

In London, immigrants can barely be called a minority. A third of the capital's population is born abroad. No one sees this more than the Catholic Church, and especially the 40-odd Catholic parishes and schools which belong to London Citizens. Go to any Central London Catholic church on a Sunday, and you are struck by the numbers, and diversity, of its congregation. In other denominations – the black evangelical congregations of South London, or inner-city Anglican parishes – the diversity is less marked, but the immigrant presence just as strong.

Some are professionals. Many are wealthy. But very large numbers are working in the capital's low-paid sector, unskilled or barely skilled, paid the national minimum wage or just above it.[2] A massive 90 per cent of London's unskilled jobs are done by migrants. Many are irregular, and vulnerable to exploitation. A London Citizens Summer Academy report in 2006 found that '[cleaning] agencies such as Ocean and KGB purpose-fully employ irregular migrants. Workers are commonly underpaid or not at all, and are then threatened with being turned over to immigration authorities if they complain. Workers employed by Ocean estimate that they are owed tens of thousands of pounds in unpaid wages.'

Irregular migrants divide into two categories: visa overstayers – people who have entered the country legally but overstayed, or had fallen into illegality after the immigration rules changed – and refused asylum-seekers, working in the shadow economy to stave off destitution. Together they make up a stable population of around more than half a million people. Yet their existence, until the Strangers into Citizens campaign drew public attention to it, has been barely acknowledged in public policy.

Although all are what newspapers describe as 'illegal immigrants' the description is inaccurate. In most cases, they have not evaded border controls to arrive. In the case of the 300–400,000 refused asylum-seekers, they have spent many years (typically 8–10 years) waiting on the process-ing of their claims, and have put down roots in the UK. Visa overstayers, too, have often been ensnared in bureaucratic processes which, on the government's own admission, have been unfit for purpose. In early 2009, for example, the UK Borders Agency (UKBA) admitted it had found 40,000 more old cases where officials had 'no formal record' of whether immigrants, many of them students, had left the country.

> *If the two parties, those who agree to leave their native land and those who agree to admit the newcomers, remain anxious to eliminate as far as possible all obstacles to the birth and growth of real confidence between the country of emigration and that of immigration, all those affected by such transference of people and places will profit by the transaction. The families will receive a plot of ground which will be native for them in the true sense of the word; the thickly inhabited countries will he relieved and their people will acquire new friends in foreign countries; and the States which receive the emigrants will acquire industrious citizens. In this way, the nations which give and those which receive will both contribute to the increased welfare of man and the progress of human culture.*[3]

Britain's irregular resident population began to build up around 2001, when there was something close to a collapse in the Home Office's ability to process a huge rise in asylum claims. Yet this is far from being a symptom of bureaucratic dysfunction alone. The large irregular presence also reflects the state's difficulty in catching up with the movement of people (along with goods and capital) in an age of globalisation, when the combination of cheap travel and instability and poverty around the world have led to a historically unprecedented displacement of people, coinciding with a concentration of capital in wealthy countries leading to a demand for labour in an expanding economy. The stable, long-term, resident undocumented population in the United States, for example, is close to 12 million; in the EU as a whole it is reckoned to be around 5 million. The UK's share of that number was estimated in 2006 at 430,000; recently, the LSE has conducted research which revises that number upwards to 618,000, of whom 442,000 are in London.[4]

The response of the state to this large, resident population living outside the law has been consistently one of denial. To admit that half a million 'resident aliens' are rooted in UK society and incapable of being removed would be – the government believes – politically disastrous. So both government and opposition cling to the myth that 'illegal immigrants should go home' and are being 'dealt with' through tough immigration enforcement policies. It is a fiction.

Meanwhile, civil society bears the cost of caring for this 'shadow' population.

London Citizens found itself drawn into the issue through two of its existing campaigns. Efforts to secure a living wage for London's cleaners and low-paid workers revealed the presence of a large number of refused asylum-seekers living in the capital, vulnerable to destitution or exploitation in illegal jobs, often exploited by unscrupulous agencies. It was clear that the root cause of this misery and exploitation – the lack of legal status of long-term irregular migrants – would need to be tackled. Meanwhile, through its campaign to improve conditions at the Lunar House immigrant processing centre in Croydon, described later in this chapter, South London Citizens had gathered compelling evidence of chaos at the heart of the immigration system.

It was time for civil society to call upon the state to act.

Mass for Migrant Workers

In January 2006 London Citizens approached the office of the Archbishop of Westminster, Cardinal Cormac Murphy-O'Connor, to propose a Mass for Migrant Workers and a church report into their conditions.

The Cardinal agreed, conscious of the similarities between his own time and that of Cardinal Manning – when London was swelled by the presence of poor Irish labourers living in slums who, then as now, looked to the Church for support and protection. A report was commissioned, and a date for the Mass was fixed for the May Bank Holiday that year, to be celebrated on the Feast of St Joseph the Worker. It has been an annual fixture ever since.[5]

Many factors led to Cardinal Murphy-O'Connor's decision to call at that Mass for a conditional regularisation programme: the evidence from his own parishes of the exploitation of vulnerable migrants, reports from the front line of the London Citizens living-wage campaign, inspiration from papal declarations on the obligation to respect the dignity of undocumented migrants, the example of the US bishops, who had long called for a means for irregular migrants to regularise their status, as well as a report by a think tank published just weeks before the Mass for Migrant Workers, which contained findings that would be defining for the campaign.[6]

The first Mass for Migrant Workers, organised by London Citizens in collaboration with the three Catholic dioceses of London and its many ethnic chaplaincies, was unforgettable. More than 2,000 migrants from the three Dioceses packed the side aisles of the Cathedral, bursting into applause after the Cardinal's homily and at various points in the Mass. Many were in tears. 'We hope that this Mass will communicate to you that, as far as the Catholic Church is concerned, you are Londoners,' the Cardinal told them. 'We want you to feel welcome in our parishes and our schools and our ethnic chaplaincies. We want you to know that you belong.'

The Mass was a vision of Pentecost – music from Africa, Latin America and Poland, readings and prayers in Malayalam, Lebanese, Spanish, Lithuanian and Chinese, and parish banners from across London stacked alongside those of ethnic associations. A group of Africans presented the gifts in a stunning mixture of gentle dance and choral praise. The Alleluia was sung by Brazilians in Portuguese.

In his homily, the Cardinal quoted Pope John Paul II's 1979 migration day message: 'The Church is the place where illegal immigrants are also recognised and welcomed as brothers and sisters.' He told the congregation that the Church did not encourage or approve of illegal immigration, and believed in border controls; but nor could the Church ignore the plight of people without legal status who had put down roots in the UK.

'While our nation benefits economically from the presence of undocumented workers, too often we turn a blind eye when they are exploited by employers,' he said, adding: 'Is it not time to consider, as other countries have done, ways of regularising their situation – those who are working in the country and do not have a criminal record – to the benefit of our economy and to enable them to play a fuller part in society?'

In an interview with the BBC *Sunday* programme, Cardinal Murphy-O'Connor answered criticism from Migration Watch UK that he appeared to be encouraging illegal immigration. 'It is for the Government – and we would support the Government – to ensure that illegal immigration is not allowed,' he said. 'That is their responsibility. But once they're here, as a Christian I have to say: "I stand with you." Even if they're here illegally, it's not for me as a Christian to say, "I am going to make sure you're deported tomorrow." It's for me to say: "What are your immediate needs? How can I stand with you and help you?" '

> *Immigration can be a resource for development rather than an obstacle to it. In the modern world, where there are still grave inequalities between rich countries and poor countries, and where advances in communication quickly reduce distances, the immigration of people looking for a better life is on the increase. These people come from less privileged areas of the earth and their arrival in developed countries is often perceived as a threat to the high levels of wellbeing achieved thanks to decades of economic growth. In most cases, however, immigrants fill a labour need which would otherwise remain unfulfilled in sectors and territories where the local workforce is insufficient or unwilling to engage in the work in question. (CSDC 297)*

Immigration in CST

Catholic social teaching on migration has many sources: papal and Roman documents, as well as documents of national bishops' conferences. The foundational papal document was Pope Pius XII's *Exsul Familia* (1952), which was summarised and added to in the Vatican II document *Gaudium et Spes* (1964). Two contemporary documents have advanced the issue: the Vatican's *Erga Migrantes Christi* (see below) and the US bishops' *Strangers No Longer* (2003), to which can be added the bishops' conference of England and Wales's 2008 *Mission to Migrants in England and Wales.*

CST has traditionally upheld both the right to migrate and a nation's right to restrict immigration, a tension that must be resolved by policy-makers in the light of the common good. According to *Gaudium et Spes*, citizens have a right to migrate (*GS* 65) just as governments also have a right to regulate a nation's borders (*GS* 87).

But CST is emphatic on the need for the dignity of migrants – whatever their circumstances, legal or illegal – to be treated as human beings, and to be welcomed and integrated. According to *Gaudium et Spes*,

> When workers come from another country or district and contribute to the economic advancement of a nation or region by their labour, all discrimination as regards wages and working conditions must be carefully avoided. All the people, moreover, above all the public authorities, must treat them not as mere tools of production but as persons, and must help them to bring their families to live with them and to provide themselves with a decent dwelling; they must also see to it that these workers are incorporated into the social life of the country or region that receives them. (*GS* 66)

Surveying the literature in Catholic social teaching on migration, the US bishops in 2003 summarised it in five core principles:

I   **Persons have the right to find opportunities in their homeland.** All persons have the right to find in their own countries the economic, political, and social opportunities to live in dignity and achieve a full life through the use of their God-given gifts. In this context, work that provides a just, living wage is a basic human need.

II   **Persons have the right to migrate to support themselves and their families.** The Church recognizes that all the goods of the earth belong to all people. When persons cannot find employment in their country of origin to support themselves and their families, they have a right to find work elsewhere in order to survive. Sovereign nations should provide ways to accommodate this right.

III   **Sovereign nations have the right to control their borders.** The Church recognizes the right of sovereign nations to control their territories but rejects such control when it is exerted merely for the purpose of acquiring additional wealth. More powerful economic nations, which have the ability to protect and feed their residents, have a stronger obligation to accommodate migration flows.

IV **Refugees and asylum seekers should be afforded protection.** Those who flee wars and persecution should be protected by the global community. This requires, at a minimum, that migrants have a right to claim refugee status without incarceration and to have their claims fully considered by a competent authority.

V   **The human dignity and human rights of undocumented migrants should be respected.** Regardless of their legal status, migrants, like all persons, possess inherent human dignity that should be respected. Often they are subject to punitive laws and harsh treatment from enforcement officers from both receiving and transit countries. Government policies that respect the basic human rights of the undocumented are necessary.[7]

In their 2008 pre-election statement, the US bishops summarised the Church's position as follows:

> The Gospel mandate to 'welcome the stranger' requires Catholics to care for and stand with immigrants, both documented and undocumented, including immigrant children. Comprehensive reform is urgently necessary to fix a broken immigration system and should include a temporary work programme with worker protections and a path to permanent residency; family reunification policies; a broad and fair legalisation programme; access to legal protections, including due process and essential public programmes; refuge for those fleeing persecution and exploitation; and policies to address the root causes of migration. The right and responsibility of nations to control their borders and to maintain the rule of law should be recognised. (Faithful Citizenship 83)

In their teaching on migration of April 2008, the Catholic bishops of England and Wales summarised CST on the issue in three principles:

- People have a right to migrate to sustain their lives and the lives of their families.
- A country has the right to regulate its borders and control migration.
- A country must regulate its borders with justice and mercy, and recognise and respect the human dignity and rights of migrants.

Like the US bishops, they advocated regularisation for those who had put down roots.

> While most migrants are in Britain with permission, many are 'undocumented'. Sometimes this is because they have entered the

country illegally, but in most cases, it is because they have overstayed their visas or where their asylum claims have failed but they cannot return, because their countries are still in turmoil or refuse to accept their return. Many of these migrants have been here for several years; some have even set down roots and started families. Without condoning illegal immigration, the Church's position on this, as in other fields of human endeavour, does not allow economic, social and political calculations to prevail over the person, but on the contrary, for the dignity of the human person to be put above everything else, and the rest to be conditioned by it. The Church will continue to advocate compassion to allow the 'undocumented' an opportunity to acquire proper status, so that they can continue to contribute to the common good without the constant fear of discovery and removal ... In making this call, the Church upholds the sacredness of life, the value of family life and the dignity of labour – principles that are central to Catholic Social Teaching.[8]

A proposal for the common good

The Mass inspired London Citizens' Strangers into Citizens campaign, which was launched at the TELCO assembly in November 2006 with supportive video messages from both the Cardinal and the Mayor of London. South London Citizens and, the following year, West London Citizens, both voted for a campaign that would make the case for a selective, conditional amnesty which would enable around 400,000 visa overstayers and refused asylum-seekers who had been resident for more than four years to gain access to citizenship through a two-year pathway scheme.

The proposal was for a conditional, 'earned' amnesty. It reflected the need for a country to protect its borders, and to maintain immigration controls, while at the same time recognising that a person who puts down roots acquires rights over time which eclipse that legal requirement. Behind the six-year 'pathway' to citizenship was an important moral principle that the state's moral right to deport erodes over time. It was admitted by the Home Office that it was impossible and unrealistic forcibly to remove hundreds of thousands of people; that concession led, logically, to a pathway into citizenship, the alternative to which was to live with a large population outside the law, to the detriment of society as a whole. Added to this pragmatic case was the moral wrong in forcing someone to leave a place where they have lived for a long time, and the benefit to the state – demonstrated by a Spanish regularisation programme in 2005 – of allowing a large number of people to pay taxes and contribute as law-abiding citizens.

But at the heart of the proposal was a firm CST principle. A pathway into citizenship for people who had put down roots was implicitly recognising that human beings are persons, who over time form links and relationships, and cannot be treated as commodities, or condemned to a furtive existence by their legal status as non-persons.[9] Yet its resident requirement avoided the errors of a radical cosmopolitanism – too much openness to the outsider – which can undermine a nation's integrity. A conditional amnesty with too liberal conditions would undermine border controls. The Strangers into Citizens proposal is careful to ensure that a regularisation would not have a 'green-light' effect on further illegal immigration.

Strangers into Citizens is inspired by CST in another, key way: it emphasises not just justice for migrants themselves — unable to defend their rights by access to the law – but the common good, what is right and good for society as a whole. Nobody benefits by keeping half a million people in legal limbo: it undermines minimum-wage legislation, encourages the shadow economy, makes a mockery of the law, deprives the state of taxes and thousands of people of their dignity – while leaving civil society to pick up the pieces and bear the costs. Against each of these disadvantages, regularisation brings a corresponding benefit: for the British workers and businesses undercut by illegal working practices; for the law, undermined by being so out of synch with reality; for the Exchequer, which would benefit from unpaid tax revenues; and for the sake of the state, which was being undermined by the presence outside it of a substantial population unrecognised by the law. It was the right thing – the *only* right thing – to do.

> Our society should no longer tolerate a status quo that perpetuates a permanent underclass of persons and benefits from their labour without offering them legal protections ... As a moral matter, we must resolve the legal status of those who are here without proper documentation so they can fully contribute their talents to our nation's economic, social and spiritual wellbeing.[10]

The campaign has mobilised hundreds of civil-society organisations across the UK, mostly small, volunteer-run, and based in churches and mosques, which daily offer crucial humanitarian support to refused asylum seekers and other irregular migrants facing destitution. The number of these organisations and the dedication of those who worked in them are powerful testimony to the scale of the problem,[11] as well as to the commitment of civil society to relieving their plight. These organisations are the real strength of Strangers into Citizens; their experience, and the burden they carry – a burden which, as long as the Government refuses to regularise, is effectively imposed on faith organisations and charities – is what has given the campaign its moral legitimacy. And it was these organisations which were able to help migrants articulate their stories, stories which contradicted the media portrayal of outsiders taking advantage of British hospitality and resources.

> *We are thinking of the precarious situation of a great number of emigrant workers whose condition as foreigners makes it all the more difficult for them to make any sort of social vindication, in spite of their real participation in the economic effort of the country that receives them. It is urgently necessary for people to go beyond a narrowly nationalist attitude in their regard and to give them a charter which will assure them a right to emigrate, favour their integration, facilitate their professional advancement and give them access to decent housing where, if such is the case, their families can join them. Linked to this category are the people who, to find work, or to escape a disaster or a hostile climate, leave their regions and find themselves without roots among other people.*
>
> *It is everyone's duty, but especially that of Christians, to work with energy for the establishment of universal brotherhood, the indispensable basis for authentic justice and the condition for enduring peace: 'We cannot in truthfulness call upon that God who is the Father of all if we refuse to act in a brotherly way toward certain men, created to God's image. A man's relationship with God the Father and his relationship with his brother men are so linked together that Scripture says: "He who does not love does not know God" (I Jn. 4, 8).' (OA 17)*

Thousands gathered under Strangers into Citizens banners on 7 May 2007 in Trafalgar Square following the second Mass for Migrant Workers at Westminster Cathedral. Among those addressing the rally were the (Catholic) Archbishop of Westminster, the (Anglican) Bishop of Southwark, the head of the Muslim Council of Britain, a representative of the Chief Rabbi, as well as assorted peers, MPs and trade unionists. Coachloads came from across the country as dozens of small organisations, often attached to faith congregations, were mobilised to show their support.

> No country can be expected to address today's problems of migration by itself. We are all witnesses of the burden of suffering, the dislocation and the aspirations that accompany the flow of migrants. The phenomenon, as everyone knows, is difficult to manage; but there is no doubt that foreign workers, despite any difficulties concerning integration, make a significant contribution to the economic development of the host country through their labour, besides that which they make to their country of origin through the money they send home. Obviously, these labourers cannot be considered as a commodity or a mere workforce. They must not, therefore, be treated like any other factor of production. Every migrant is a human person who, as such, possesses fundamental, inalienable rights that must be respected by everyone and in every circumstance. (CV 62)

The event had an impact on public opinion, puncturing the official silence over the issue which politicians were anxious to maintain. London Citizens' leaders and organisers debated MigrationWatch with government officials on television and radio throughout the day. In the *Guardian*, Madeleine Bunting praised London Citizens for daring to take on an issue everyone wanted to brush under the carpet;[12] editorials endorsing the idea appeared in the *Independent, The Tablet, The Universe*, and the *Voice* as well as the *Observer*, the *Daily Telegraph*, and the *Spectator*. Some argued from a moral or justice standpoint, others from a pragmatic point of view – the impossibility of mass deportations and the financial and social benefits of regularisation. Only the *Daily Express* and the *Daily Mail* remained steadfastly opposed, claiming – in ignorance of the evidence gathered by the campaign – that regularisation would attract more illegal immigrants and cost the country billions.[13] An independent poll commissioned by the campaign found only 31 per cent of British people favoured deporting people who had lived in the UK for more than four years and were paying taxes. The poll showed that British public opinion was generally favourable to the idea of a pathway into citizenship for long-term migrants, and was not noticeably different from public opinion in the US, where even swing voters favour comprehensive action on immigration over 'enforcement-only' policies by a margin of 60 to 40.14

A broad-based organisation such as London Citizens is broad in both senses: in its make-up, and in the issues it chooses to tackle. It is a vehicle for social change, in that it draws upon thousands of relationships formed in the heat of earlier battles – relationships with politicians and businesses, as well as the bonds among the people of the member organisations of London Citizens.

These relationships now paid off in getting Strangers into Citizens endorsed and recognised by politicians. Dozens of MPs in all the main parties signed an Early Day Motion, and the campaign was backed by three out of six of the candidates to the deputy leadership of the Labour Party in April that year. At the time of writing, six London councils have passed motions in support, as has the GLA. In June 2007 the Strangers into Citizens' proposal was debated in the House of Commons. 'Maintaining the current policy is causing chaos, distress, bureaucratic logjams and misery on a large scale,' said the Catholic MP Jon Cruddas, who went on to list the many benefits of regularisation.[15] After meeting with campaigners, the Liberal Democrat Party came out in favour, adopting, in September 2007, the idea of 'an earned route to citizenship' but with ten years' residence conditions.[16]

In April 2008 the Catholic bishops of England and Wales formally endorsed regularisation. Without condoning illegal immigration, they said, 'the Church will continue to advocate compassion to allow the "undocumented" an opportunity to acquire proper status, so that they can continue to contribute to the common good without the constant fear of discovery and removal'.[17]

In the same month, London Citizens mounted a large assembly at Methodist Central Hall, in which the leading candidates for Mayor of London were challenged to agree to a four-point agenda, including Strangers into Citizens and the London Living Wage. To the surprise of many, the victor of that contest, Boris Johnson, agreed to both. He has since done more than any other politician to advance the case for Strangers into Citizens, making the case on a Channel 4 *News* interview which attracted the scorn of the *Daily Mail*.[18] In the same interview, he announced that he had commissioned research from the LSE into the costs and benefits of regularisation.

In March 2009, the Mayor took part in a BBC *Panorama* programme which examined the issues raised by the campaign. 'If it does look as though they could make a contribution to society, we should regularise their status or offer them the chance of regularising their status', he said, as long as they have been resident 'for a considerable period of time'. He acknowledged regularisation was a 'hard political argument to win' but he had been convinced by London Citizens' case. 'If people are going to be here and we've chronically failed to kick them out it's morally right that they should contribute in their taxes to the rest of society,' he told the BBC.[19]

On 4 May 2009, the second Strangers into Citizens rally brought together nearly twice the number of two years before – this time following services not just at Westminster Cathedral but at Westminster Abbey and Westminster Central Hall.

In June, the LSE published its long-awaited report into the costs and benefits of a conditional regularisation for undocumented migrants who had been resident for more than five years.[20] It dismissed fears that the move would fuel further large-scale illegal immigration, arguing that Britain's much-tightened border controls would nowadays be a sufficient deterrent. Far from being a financial burden, it concluded, 'this new research has found an amnesty could be worth up to £3bn a year to the country's economy'. Boris Johnson said it would amount to 'negligence' at a time of recession not to introduce a 'time-limited and earned amnesty for hard-working migrants who demonstrate a commitment to contributing fully to our society'.

Strangers into Citizens had led not just to a powerful moral and humanitarian case for regularisation, but an economic case too. It had won the argument, although not – at the time of writing – the politics. Both the Labour and Conservative parties, fearful of a public backlash, have restated their opposition to the idea. But behind the scenes, politicians in all parties who are convinced of the merits of the case have championed Strangers into Citizens.

The campaign has transformed the climate of discussion on the issue, and pressured the government into granting permission to remain to tens of thousands of refused asylum-seekers. The letters they have received from the Home Office inform them that Leave to Remain is being granted 'because of your long association with the UK' – precisely the Strangers into Citizens argument. Although the government insist that they are resolving the huge backlog of applications 'on a case-by-case basis', some detect in the move an 'amnesty by stealth' – insufficient and arbitrary, perhaps, but proof of the campaign's impact.

Jacob and Ramoz

'Oh, Jacob will do that,' I remember being told when I first arrived at St Ignatius parish in Stamford Hill, 'he's always happy to help.' Jacob was well known in the parish. He was an usher at the Sunday Masses and helped to serve the teas and coffees afterwards. An exuberant young man in his early thirties, he had arrived from Nigeria on a student visa 15 years before. One day, I received a call from a solicitor telling me that Jacob was being detained and prepared for deportation. Three days later, despite our best efforts to intervene, he had gone.

It was long after Jacob's departure that the story emerged of his undocumented status in the UK. Only a few trusted friends – parishioners – had known of his shadow existence. He had overstayed his student visa by twelve years and in that time had changed address eight times, frightened that anything too permanent might lead to detection by immigration authorities. He had been detained five years before and had avoided deportation, but since that time had been required to register every Monday at an immigration office. He worked illegally as a part-time security guard on the other side of London, and did various cleaning and dishwashing jobs in the early mornings and late evenings. As the eldest of ten children, he would send his family a substantial amount of his earnings each month. His father had passed away during Jacob's time in the UK and was buried without his eldest son's presence because Jacob couldn't leave the country. His aged mother and aunt depended on the remittance sent home every month, and many of his younger siblings had been educated on the strength of it.

Jacob's story, although unique, is not exceptional. I have heard many others describe how they live in fear of being found out or 'picked up', and how they are exploited in the workplace. Ramoz, from Brazil, appeared at the front door of the Presbytery one morning after reading the noticeboard in the Church. He wanted to know about the poster he had seen there advocating 'Strangers into Citizens'. He listened intently as I explained the campaign, initiated by the Citizen Organising Foundation (London Citizens), for the regularisation of long-term migrants. I explained that St Ignatius Church, being very much a migrant parish and situated in a relatively poor part of the capital, had some parishioners and neighbours who were undocumented. It is important, I told him, for us as a parish to express our solidarity with the undocumented and to do everything we can to help them attain legal status in the UK.

Having sensed that this was a safe place, Ramoz disclosed that he himself 'lived in the shadows', and had done for almost nine years. It is difficult to trust people, he explained, as he expressed his relief at finding someone – a priest – who could listen to his story. Ramoz, like Jacob, had three jobs. Early each morning he travelled to the City to clean the offices of a prestigious finance company before going to work in a coffee bar for six hours. From 8 p.m. until midnight he delivered takeaway pizzas in North London. Ramoz was distressed because he had not received payment from his cleaning job for six weeks. His manager, as well as refusing to pay him, had told him not to go back again. 'But what can I do?' Ramoz asked. 'He knows I don't have any papers.' The implications of this are enormous because, as well as going unpaid, Ramoz had to change his address. He felt vulnerable because his former manager knew where he lived and, if he wanted to, could tip off the authorities. He described living in such a way that you must always be watching your back, whilst acknowledging the danger of becoming paranoid. It is easy to imagine that everyone knows your status – people you live with or even strangers walking down the street. He grimaced as he recalled the time when two policemen walked into the coffee bar and joined the queue. 'I almost fainted,' he said, 'I started sweating and could hardly speak because I thought they had come to get me.' Thankfully they ordered two coffees to take away and left …

For many migrants the Church offers a link with the past, a sort of continuity with something familiar and lasting. For these reasons, some come back to the Church after having left it years before in their home country; they find they need it in a way that they didn't at home. In coming back, they find a sense of belonging and community and, in some cases, a new sense of purpose. For undocumented migrants in particular, the Church and other religious institutions offer a safe space. 'It is the place I can be myself,' a young Cameroonian man told me recently, 'where I can sit before God and feel OK. He doesn't care whether I'm legal or not.' There are no 'illegals' to God, no borders here.

These sentiments seem to be shared by other migrants. The Ground of Justice, the Von Hugel Institute's report on the needs of migrants in London's Catholic community, found that for many the Church was like a 'home away from home.' 'Many', it says, regard the Church as a 'refuge, a harbour of hope and worship, where the idea of a Eucharistic feast is also grounded in lived community.' This seemed to be what Ramoz was getting at when he said: 'I come to Church to get nourished and to feel that I belong to something bigger. I can pray for my family in Brazil and it helps me forget my situation.'

Ramoz and other undocumented migrants like him carry a heavy burden. Not only may they suffer exploitation in the workplace and exclusion from many forms of civic life, but they experience the paralysing fear of being found out or of being betrayed by colleagues or friends – and on top of this they carry the huge expectations of their families back in their home country. Almost all of those that I have met have been sending money home whilst struggling to keep a roof over their heads in London and to feed themselves, cover their bills and travel costs. Many of them share small bedsits with three or four others and arrange sleeping times around one another's working schedules. They work in jobs that offer no entitlements to sick pay or holiday and, as Ramoz learned, can be quickly and often painfully terminated. An undocumented person's life, I have come to discover, is characterised by insecurity and a constant feeling of being dependent upon and therefore vulnerable to an assortment of external forces.

A pathway to citizenship like that proposed by Strangers into Citizens, which allows the undocumented who have lived 'in the shadows' for four years or longer to come out into the light and declare their presence, would alleviate much of this burden ...

The conditions in which many of the undocumented are forced to live and work are an infringement on their human dignity, the dignity that is repeatedly highlighted and celebrated in Catholic Social Teaching. Surely one cannot ignore a situation in which the vulnerable are continuously exploited and silenced through their own fear? This is a problem that, if not addressed, will undermine any attempt to build meaningful local communities and a cohesive society ...

On Bank Holiday Monday, 4 May 2009, a group of parishioners from St Ignatius Church joined Catholics from around London and from other parts of the country at Westminster Cathedral for a Mass for Migrants. Simultaneously, five other religious services took place in central London. The congregations, representing an assortment of Christian denominations and other faiths, joined together at the end of their respective services and marched to Trafalgar Square where, with other civic and community groups, trade unionists, Members of Parliament and interested individuals, they rallied for Strangers into Citizens. All of the different groups present are likely to have had with them, known or unknown, people like Jacob and Ramoz: undocumented, vulnerable migrants living precarious lives in the shadows of British society. Perhaps, for once, they felt valued, not only for the contribution they make to the economic and civic life of the city and nation, but for simply being who they are: our sisters and brothers. A sense of belonging that *is rooted in this knowledge and manifested through acts of shared worship and solidarity will endure, and upon that we will make strangers into citizens.*

Fr James Conway SJ, a member of the Parish Team at St Ignatius,
Stamford Hill

A human welcome: the Lunar House story

At a meeting in early 2004, the parish priest of St Dominic's Catholic Church in Croydon, Fr Ian Knowles, shared with South London Citizens lead organiser Bernadette Farrell what seemed then an extraordinary story. It turned out to be all too ordinary.

One of Fr Ian's parishioners had been battling to persuade Lunar House in Croydon, the 20-storey home of the Home Office's Immigration and Nationality Directorate (IND), that they had her visa. Lunar House is the IND's main processing centre where migrants apply for refugee status or citizenship.

Mary Apragas, a Sri Lankan woman, had spent many hours in fruitless phone calls, queuing at Lunar House in the cold, pleading with officials, but had been told over and again that *she* had her visa, and there was nothing they could do. Desperate, she had turned to her parish priest.

'What made Fr Ian angry was that because her English wasn't great her son had to go with her to Lunar House – but even then they hadn't taken her seriously,' Bernadette recalls. 'They told her they had sent their visa to her, but all she had received was an empty envelope. It wasn't until the MP got involved the visa had reappeared as if by magic. Fr Ian had made endless phone calls and been stonewalled at every turn. He was angry. He wondered how many other people went through the same experience as Mary.'

Bernadette Farrell got in touch with union officials at Lunar House, who told her of the immense frustration of the staff working in a demoralised, chaotic environment. She brought them together with Mary Apragas and her son. One union representative told him: 'I'd like to apologise on behalf of the staff for the way your mother was treated.'

'It was so powerful, the feeling in the room,' recalls Bernadette. 'That reconciliation was the catalyst for the next step. We did action research, we went to other communities, we asked them for their stories. And at a big public meeting we asked how many people here have had an experience at Lunar House. The whole room went silent and then almost every hand went up. The stories tumbled forth. What we heard convinced us that what had happened to Mary was typical – the tip of the iceberg. We felt then we had to act.'

At a South London Citizens assembly In November 2004, 400 people from SLC member institutions heard testimonies and voted to carry out a citizens' enquiry into Lunar House. The next month, commissioners were appointed, including a Catholic auxiliary bishop of Southwark, Charles Henderson, and the canon theologian of Westminster Abbey, the Revd Prof. Nicholas Sagovsky. In February 2005, the enquiry began with a public hearing at which ordinary people as well as voluntary organisations submitted evidence about how the immigration processing centre operated, highlighting the endless queues, the demoralised staff, the unaccountable systems, the inefficiency, and the cold, dreary physical conditions.

'That one reporting centre covers everything – a huge area of immigration law – yet they had people there with one o-level, who can't spell the countries people come from,' recalls Bernadette. 'You need training in immigration law to make those kinds of decisions. So we were taking on the whole culture.'

They sent letters to Lunar House and the Home Office to inform them of the enquiry, but were ignored. No surprise there: dozens of charities and campaign organisations had fruitlessly called upon Lunar House over the years to address the dysfunctional culture that prevailed there. But they were powerless.

A community-organising maxim holds that change only comes about when pressure or threat of pressure is applied. Power-holders usually resist change. To break through that impasse, the power has to be in some way taken away from them.

Sometimes banner-waving demonstrations can be effective – in the right place, at the right time. But because they are the first resort of activists without any real power base, they can also be easily dismissed by the holders of power who know, from experience, that after a short time the crowd will disperse and normality resume. A demonstration by activists can be as much an expression of powerlessness as it is of power.

Much more effective is for ordinary citizens to do the hard graft of collecting evidence, demonstrating by their efficiency and competence their commitment to the welfare of an organisation, rather than simply expressing their loathing of it. Faithful citizens care about the common good, not in partisan point-scoring.

'Make your enemy live up to their rule book' is a community-organising maxim. Every Civil Service department likes to think of itself as efficient, humane and fair-minded, working for the public good. Confronted with irrefutable evidence that it is not, it has no choice but to react – or spurn its own rule book. South London Citizens needed to hold Lunar House to its own stated values.

The team devised an official-looking questionnaire for staff, asking about their conditions. 'As they came in that morning, we told them who we were and why we there, and we asked them to fill in the form. That morning an email went out to the staff saying, "don't respond to this". But the sweet part was, we got a lot of responses, sent through the internal mail.'

In May 2005, South London Citizens parked a Winnebago outside Lunar House for three days, serving teas and coffees and conducting a systematic survey of the migrant users' experiences of Lunar House. They gathered hundreds of testimonies.

'That's when it started to change. Going to the directors of the IND armed with all this felt very different than it would have done going in at the beginning saying, "Here we are, the do-gooders"', Bernadette recalls. 'They knew by now how serious we were, that we weren't some pressure group coming at one angle. The member institutions of South London Citizens who were leading this were their neighbours. We represented their workers. We represented their users. We represented the migrants and refugees, the teachers, clergy and imams – we were broad, and they began to listen to us. It was almost like two armies coming into this building – they came in from one side, we came in from the other. And there was real recognition.'

South London Citizens planned a major hearing at the House of Lords. But the IND stalled, saying they had other appointments that day.

Bernadette went to a public talk given by the director responsible for asylum, Jeremy Oppenheim, and confronted him. 'This was just a couple of weeks before our scheduled meeting at the House of Lords, which they had known about for six months. I was angry by this stage that they hadn't committed to coming, so after Mr Oppenheim's talk I stood up and said: "We're South London Citizens. As you know, we have been holding an enquiry into Lunar House, the conditions of your staff and the experience of your users. We have a meeting in the House of Lords in two weeks' time. Will you come and hear our concerns?". He promised he would, and to bring other important staff. He kept his word. Two weeks later there we were, sitting at the House of Lords, and our commissioners asked questions to the directors of the immigration department. It was very powerful.'

Oppenheim became an important ally. Over time, he would agree to all of the recommendations of the Lunar House enquiry.

The commissioners began taking evidence for what would turn out to be a detailed, systematic report into the failures and culture of dysfunction at Lunar House. They found that 'minimum standards of comfort afforded to British citizens do not apply to migrants waiting for services at Lunar House', and listed among its areas of immediate concern the quality of facilities for applicants, the quality and fairness of transactions, the quality of IT and record keeping and the working conditions of staff. They made a series of recommendations which were published in a report that was ratified by a South London Citizens assembly in October 2005.[21]

Lunar House officials began meeting with the commissioners, and to implement changes. 'We organised visits, and they would take us round, and show us the changes they had made,' says Bernadette. 'They didn't always admit that it was because of our recommendations, but we knew they were.'

The enquiry grew bigger, as other campaign groups that had been working fruitlessly for years to get changes made at Lunar House added their evidence to SLC's.

'It was clear that in the asylum-screening process there was a real culture of disbelief – the very layout of the place, with metal bars which people had to stand between for hours, holding babies, having arrived from detention centres or airports, often hungry – and if they leaned on the railings, they were shouted at.' Bernadette Farrell continues: 'The best moment for me was when we were taken round one time and, following our recommendations, saw they had taken down the railings. It was a huge thing, a symbolic thing – that we had succeeded in shifting the culture.'

The Friends of Lunar House was established. Volunteers from SLC member parishes – parishioners, religious sisters and priests – began giving out refreshments and advice to migrants queuing in the asylum-screening unit, where they had often arrived from detention centres or days on the road without eating. Hospitality to the stranger is not just about securing dignified conditions and legal status. It is also about befriending and welcoming in acts of charity. The two, as Pope Benedict made clear in *Caritas in Veritate*, are inseparable.

A new head of Lunar House, Lin Homer, was appointed in August 2005 and came to the SLC autumn assembly two months later, promising to act on the report. The following year she took the stage at SLC's autumn 2006 assembly to make herself and her department accountable in a remarkable way – by showing a DVD they had made showcasing the improvements both to the physical layout and the way staff treated clients. The report's recommendations were ticked off, one by one.

Change requires commitment – a willingness to stick with an objective. It is here that the relationships forged by London Citizens through its one-to-ones and common actions on local issues paid off.

'The challenge was to win their respect and be taken seriously,' Bernadette says. 'We had to show we weren't coming in with an axe to grind. We were just as concerned about their own staff as about the users of Lunar House. They were impressed with the quality of our research – and the fact that we kept going back, scheduling meetings. They didn't usually act until just before the meetings, but without them they wouldn't have acted. They had to take us seriously.'

In 2008 Tony Smith, regional director for London and the South East for what was now called the UK Borders Authority (UKBA), attended the SLC autumn assembly in Battersea. Eleanor Sharpton, one of the report's commissioners, reminded him that there was one outstanding recommendation from the enquiry – a covered waiting area at Lunar House. The assembly's co-chair asked him if he would agree, but Smith prevaricated, unsure if he could secure the budget.

But in January 2009, Smith met the SLC team to announce he had secured £800,000 funding for the new Welcome Centre, and invited SLC to be involved in the plans, meeting every two months to review progress. The new Centre, with seating, heating and a welcome desk, replaces a cold, cheerless area known as the 'cattle shed', and allows Lunar House finally to receive migrants as human beings.

After the meeting, the UKBA officials told Bernadette Farrell this could never have been achieved without SLC's pressure. 'It's what we wanted to happen, but it would never have got it through without you holding us to it,' they told her.

The new Centre was unveiled on 21 December 2009, when South London Citizens gathered, once again, to sing carols, and bring to a formal close the Lunar House enquiry. The Centre bears a plaque commemorating the Sri Lankan woman, now dead, whose story sparked it all. The plaque says simply:

MARY APRAGAS 2004. VOICE OF COURAGE.

Restoring sanctuary

The Lunar House enquiry had exposed remarkable iniquities and injustices at the heart of Britain's asylum system, not least the use of destitution as a policy of deterrence – a policy described by the Catholic MP Iain Duncan-Smith as 'nasty and mean' as well as counter-productive.[22]

In 2007, CitizensUK launched an Independent Asylum Commission (IAC), headed by a retired judge and backed by the Archbishop of Canterbury, to hold public hearings across the UK into the treatment of asylum-seekers. The IAC found that 280,000 'refused' asylum-seekers in the UK were living in poverty and destitution, unable to access benefits, and banned from working, yet who had no realistic prospect of returning to their countries. The IAC made 180 recommendations in three reports published in 2008.

Asylum system 'Shameful for UK'

The UK's treatment of asylum seekers falls 'seriously below' the standards of a civilised society, a report says.

The Independent Asylum Commission, led by an ex-senior judge, said the system denied sanctuary to some in need and failed to remove others who should go.

It said the treatment of some asylum seekers was a shameful blemish on the UK's international reputation.

But the Border and Immigration Agency has rejected the report, claiming it operates a 'firm but humane' system.

The commission spent a year researching the report and spoke to former home secretaries, policy makers and asylum seekers.

It was established in the wake of calls from community organisations and charities for an authoritative examination of asylum after former Home Secretary John Reid branded the immigration system 'not fit for purpose'.

Sir John Waite, co-chairman of the commission and a former Appeal Court judge, said this particular issue was a 'blemish' on the UK's reputation.

The report praised immigration officials for recent reforms to how they manage asylum applications – but it warned that a 'culture of disbelief' was leading to 'perverse and unjust decisions'.

> *The commissioners said policymakers were at times using 'indefensible' threats of destitution to try to force some asylum seekers to leave the UK.*
>
> *Another commission member, Lord Ramsbotham, a former chief inspector of prisons, told the BBC that officials considering asylum claims often had a poor understanding of an individual's circumstances.*
>
> *'We are concerned at the level of the treatment of children, the treatment of women, the treatment of those with health needs, particularly mental health needs, torture survivors.'*
>
> *'We are a country with a basic instinct of fair play – it's rooted deeply in our national character,' Sir John told the BBC.*
>
> *'The system denies fair play to asylum seekers not out of malice but because of a lack of resources.'* [23]

After the IAC's interim findings were published in March 2008, it was a lead story on the *Today* programme, BBC TV evening news, and the major national newspapers. The action is in the reaction – and the media play a powerful role in bringing that about.

'Up to that point the UKBA had agreed to respond to the interim findings, but weren't taking it very seriously,' says Jonathan Cox, IAC co-ordinator and now lead organiser of the Citizens for Sanctuary campaign.

'We gave them an advance copy to make sure they could respond to the media coverage, but they didn't think there would be much, and clearly didn't brief senior officials. When we were on the *Today* programme, the UKBA was forced to respond. By the end of the evening the story was building to the point where they had to wheel out the immigration minister, Liam Byrne. Their response had moved from, "this is a report we had nothing to do with" to having to respond directly to what the report said.'

Caught in the media headlights, the UKBA's response to the IAC changed. At the launch of each of the reports, they sent senior officials who then promised to meet with Citizens teams to discuss their implementation.

Citizens for Sanctuary is a London Citizens/CitizensUK campaign to persuade government to implement the IAC's 180 recommendations. [24]

The name is significant. One of its objectives is to restore the idea of sanctuary, phasing out the term 'asylum', with its connotations of madness and – following years of tabloid stories of 'bogus' asylum-seekers – abuse and duplicity. 'Sanctuary' better expresses the idea of a holy, protected space, a hallowed place of safety where the dignity of human beings should trump narrow legal or political considerations.

Citizens for Sanctuary trains leaders in London Citizens and across the country – many of them migrants in legal limbo – to negotiate directly with those who have the power to make change. The UKBA, the Welsh Assembly, the Scottish Government and the Northern Ireland Assembly are all negotiating with 17 Citizens for Sanctuary teams around the country. The UKBA has committed to a protocol for negotiation and a timeline set by Citizens for Sanctuary to negotiate on all 180 IAC recommendations. Remarkably, they have agreed to phase out the term 'asylum' in their internal communications, replacing it with 'protection' – a shift in policy that has gone virtually unnoticed.

Citizens for Sanctuary arranges public actions, like that of January 2009 when hundreds gathered outside 10 Downing Street calling for Zimbabweans – whom the Government says it will not send back in the current political climate – to be allowed to work to save themselves from destitution. And it takes action to subvert injustices. Chief among these are the supermarket vouchers which certain people seeking sanctuary are given by Government while they await the processing of their claims. The vouchers can only be spent at supermarkets, meaning that people needing cash to make phone calls or travel are forced to sell them on the black market for less than their face value. Under the Voucher Exchange Scheme co-ordinated by Citizens for Sanctuary, London Citizens' member organisations instead buy the vouchers at face value from people seeking sanctuary, giving them the cash they need. Some £45,000 of vouchers a month were being traded at the time of writing. Says Jonathan Cox of the scheme: 'It makes a huge difference to the lives of people seeking sanctuary.'

Citizens for Sanctuary has created a pledge intended for MPs and other public figures to the principle of sanctuary, to a fairer and more effective system of deciding who has a real fear of persecution or who has not, and to a more humane treatment of those awaiting decisions – including an end to the detention of children. The pledge has been signed by the Catholic bishops of England and Wales, and an increasing number of MPs. The aim is to change a public climate which tolerates the dehumanising conditions of people seeking sanctuary.

Nothing better illustrates the inhumanity of those conditions than the children locked up for months at a time in detention centres. And what better way to spotlight this than an attempt by St Nicholas – in the company of the Canon Theologian of Westminster Abbey – to bring them Christmas presents? The *Observer* has the story:[25]

> It started out as a well-intentioned attempt to bring festive cheer to some of society's most neglected members – the hundreds of children who each year are caught up in the UK's asylum system.
>
> But when the Anglican church's leading expert on Father Christmas, dressed as St Nicholas himself, arrived with one of Britain's most distinguished clerics to distribute presents to children held at the Yarl's Wood immigration removal centre in Bedfordshire, things took a turn straight out of Dickens.
>
> An unedifying standoff developed that saw the security personnel who guard the perimeter fence prevent St Nicholas, the patron saint of children and the imprisoned, from delivering £300 worth of presents donated by congregations of several London churches.
>
> In a red robe and long white beard, clutching a bishop's mitre and crook, St Nick – in real life, the Rev Canon James Rosenthal, a world authority on St Nicholas of Myra, the inspiration for Father Christmas – gently protested that he was not a security threat, but to no avail.
>
> Then as St Nicholas, accompanied by the Rev Professor Nicholas Sagovsky, canon theologian at Westminster Abbey, attempted to bless the gifts, the increasingly angry security guards called the police. The resulting ill-tempered and surreal impasse between church and state was videotaped by asylum seeker support groups and could become an internet viral hit.
>
> The row comes amid mounting concern about the treatment of children in immigration removal centres. Last week senior doctors called for an immediate end to the 'profoundly harmful' detention of children in immigration removal centres. In today's *Observer* a number of leading children's authors – including Michael Morpurgo, Michael Bond and Philip Pullman – have signed a letter calling for an end to child detention.
>
> Rosenthal, who regularly appears alongside the Archbishop of Canterbury at festive parades, is the founder of the St Nicholas

Society, which was set up to promote 'interest, learning, and appreciation of the tradition of St Nicholas'.

'St Nick has never been turned away from anywhere before,' Rosenthal said. 'So I was extremely disappointed not to be able to hand deliver the gifts to the children detained at Yarl's Wood. I hope the kids realise that they will be firmly in my prayers.'

The St Nicholas Society, along with Citizens for Sanctuary, which campaigns to end the detention of children and families in the asylum system, is writing to the centre's management to complain at how it handled the pre-announced visit. They have complained about the heavy-handed tactics employed by the guards who patrol the perimeter fence and Serco, the private company that operates Yarl's Wood.

The two groups say that Serco refused requests to provide details about the 35 children in the centre so they could receive appropriate presents. They complain that the company did not respond to numerous requests to discuss how a handover of presents could be carried out if St Nicholas was prevented from entering during his visit this month.

Serco also refused permission for the two clerics to enter the centre to visit two refugee families later the same day, as it had previously agreed. They were handed letters from Dawn Elaine, contracts manager at Yarl's Wood, saying permission had been revoked because of 'concerns about your conduct'.

The minor row is threatening to escalate into a bigger furore over the government's policy of keeping children in Immigration Removal Centres.

'If this is how visitors are treated, I shudder to imagine what else transpires inside Yarl's Wood,' Rosenthal said.

Sagovsky added: 'This was about bringing a moment of joy to kids locked up in a deplorable situation. I can't help but contrast the smiles and wonderment on the faces of the children St Nicholas visited at a local primary school with the sad fate of those kids who will be locked up in Yarl's Wood over Christmas.'

It is estimated that 1,000 children are detained every year. Last week the Royal Colleges of Paediatrics and Child Health, alongside leading GPs, psychiatrists and the UK Faculty of Public Health, warned the detention of children and their families caused 'significant harm' and should be ended without delay.

Dr Philip Collins, a forensic adolescent psychiatrist at the South London and Maudsley NHS Foundation Trust, said children of asylum seekers were 'uniquely at risk' of 'very high levels' of mental health problems.

The organisation Medical Justice said it had seen more than 100 children in Yarl's Wood Immigration Removal Centre, and shared the doctors' concerns. The organisation's clinical director, Dr Frank Arnold, said: 'Our findings accord exactly with those of the royal colleges.

'Over the years, when challenged, the response of UK Borders Agency (UKBA), and the private company it subcontracts healthcare to, have ranged from pleading ignorance, to painting walls a different colour, to publishing a vast number of documents, which prove meaningless because the health outcomes for children seem no better, and remain frightening.'

A spokesman for Serco referred questions to the Home Office, which insists only people subject to stringent security checks can be allowed into the detention centre and there can be no exceptions.

However, it seems even the Home Office is keen to avoid being labelled Scrooge. Alan Kittle, Director of Detention Services for the UK Border Agency said: 'UKBA already has procedures in place to ensure any children held in detention over the Christmas period receive a present and get to see Santa.'

Focus on *Erga Migrantes Caritas Christi*

- This 2004 'Instruction' is from the Pontifical Council for the Pastoral Care of Migrants and Itinerant People, one of the Vatican 'pastoral' departments created after the Second Vatican Council. The fact that Pope Paul VI created a dedicated department for the Church's support for migrants is an indication of the importance CST has attached to the phenomenon of immigration. The magna carta of the Church's thinking on migration is Pope Pius XII's *Exsul Familia Nazarethana* (1952).

- 'The Love of Christ for Migrants' is intended to update Pope Paul VI's *Pastoralis migratorum cura*. A large part of the document is taken up with internal questions of how Catholics can and should support the foreign-born among them. But it also lays out basic principles of how migrants should themselves be treated and how the phenomenon of migration is to be viewed, thereby making an important contribution to CST.

- Today's migration is the 'vastest movement of people of all times' involving at least 200 million people. Emulating the love of Christ for migrants (2 Cor. 5:14), 'all Christians must respond to this challenge; it is not just a matter of good will or the personal charisma of a few' (*EMCC* 3).

- There are many causes – conflict, demography, economic imbalances – and the impact of migration is felt the world over. Migration is linked to globalisation, providing new opportunities for people to know one another, and promotes economic development. 'Many nations, in fact, would not be what they are today without the contribution made by millions of immigrants' (*EMCC* 5).

- Migration is often marked by suffering – especially of women migrants who are often contracted as unskilled labourers (or domestics) and employed illegally. Migrants are regularly deprived of their elementary human rights, and many are trafficked – 'a new chapter in the history of slavery'. Foreign workers should not be considered merchandise or merely manpower and should not be treated as a factor of production. 'Every migrant enjoys inalienable fundamental rights which must be respected in all cases.'

- The condition of migrants is 'a challenge to the faith and love of believers, who are called on to heal the evils caused by migration and discover the plan God pursues through it even when caused by obvious injustices'.

- The suffering that often accompanies migration 'is neither more nor less than the birth-pangs of a new humanity' (*EMCC* 12). Migration in the Old Testament is part of the foundation of a new society: the prophets call people out of discrimination and oppression to form a nation (*EMCC* 13). In the foreigner a Christian sees the face of Christ himself – born away from home and exiled to Egypt, and who had 'nowhere to lay his head' (Matt. 8:20). Mary is 'a living symbol of the woman emigrant' – the Madonna of the Way (*EMCC* 15).

- The Church is born of Pentecost, a symbolic meeting of peoples of all races and languages. Hospitality to foreigners and itinerants has always been a keynote of Christian attitudes towards the world. 'The peculiarities of migrants is an appeal for us to live again the fraternity of Pentecost, when differences are harmonised by the Spirit and charity becomes authentic in accepting one another' (*EMCC* 18).

- 'To this end it is important that communities do not think that they have completed their duty to migrants simply by performing acts of fraternal assistance or even by supporting legislation aimed at giving them their due place in society while respecting their identity as foreigners. Christians must in fact promote an authentic *culture of welcome* capable of accepting the truly human values of the immigrants over and above any difficulties caused by living together with persons who are different.' (*EMCC* 39).

- 'The "foreigner" is God's messenger who surprises us and interrupts the regularity and logic of daily life, bringing near those who are far away. In "foreigners" the Church sees Christ who "pitches His tent among us" (cf. *Jn* 1:14) and who "knocks at our door" (cf. *Ap* 3:20). This meeting – characterised by attention, welcome, sharing and solidarity, by the protection of the rights of migrants and of commitment to evangelise – reveals the constant solicitude of the Church, which discovers authentic values in migrants and considers them a great human resource' (*EMCC* 101).

CONCLUSION

At the end of a London Citizens action, an evaluation always begins with the question, *how do you feel?*

Faithful Citizens is an action on you. And as you know by now, 'the action is in the reaction'. So how do *you* feel? You might want to pause a few moments to find out – light a candle, perhaps.

Those feelings are important. Inspired, overwhelmed, enthused, impressed – intimidated, wary? The feelings might lead you into thinking about what you can or should do with what you have read. Which bits struck you? Which parts inspired or surprised you most?

You may wonder: what next?

You could assemble a group in your parish or school, and invite a London Citizens organiser to tell you what they do, and how they do it. And from that, it might happen, over time, that your parish or school or charity wants to join. It's a gradual process, which doesn't happen without plenty of one-to-ones.

You could begin by inviting an organiser to give you one-to-one training; and maybe your parish or school could introduce a one-to-one programme –as Fr Sean's parish did one Lent. Who knows where that could lead?

If you are a priest or pastoral assistant, you might want to imagine what London Citizens could do for your parish, helping people to become faithful citizens who see and act within the social Catholic tradition on the issues that matter to your community.

If you are a catechist, or teacher of RCIA, you may consider introducing some CST principles into your course – and illustrate it with some of the stories in this book.

If you are a parishioner, or a teacher, or someone who considers themselves quite 'ordinary', then I hope you might also see yourself as a London Citizens leader. Every achievement of London Citizens has been made possible because of people like you, working with others – and experiencing the joy of citizen politics.

You may think you've got no time to give to secure a living wage in the businesses around you, or be part of negotiations for a fairer asylum system or a community land trust. You're in good company. Most leaders in London Citizens have demanding jobs and family commitments. But they turn up to borough meetings and assemblies, or dip in and out of campaigns, because they feel energised by taking part. What London Citizens does depends on teams, so people can come and go as their timetables allow.

Maybe what's really struck you is CST. If you feel the urge to dig deeper, you could form a discussion group to study the social Catholic encyclicals, and use *Faithful Citizens* as a 'way in' to what might seem abstract or forbidding ideas. You could meet over six weeks, pre-reading a chapter before each meeting, and dipping into the list of principles in the Appendix 1.

Or you could order a copy of *Faithful Citizens* – I'm assuming you'll want to keep yours – to give to groups in your parish who already work in social action. They might be attracted to the power which London Citizens, with many years and much experience of effective social change, gives them.

But remember, the most important thing about community organising is what CST teaches us about relationships: this is the key to building the power to act. Before you can act, you must first build those relationships. Power precedes programme.

There are many ways 'in'. London Citizens holds training courses – in-house, one-day, two-day and even five-day trainings. If you live in London, almost every week there will be an 'action' or an assembly somewhere near you. Contact London Citizens and get yourself invited.

Or if you fancy a little more reading and googling, there's a list of resources in Appendix 3 for you to follow up on. The Battersea children's video, among many others, is on YouTube, ready to melt your heart.

And if you're not ready for any of this – or even if you are – it's worth pondering Pope Benedict XVI's words at the end of *Caritas in Veritate*.

> As we contemplate the vast amount of work to be done, we are sustained by our faith that God is present alongside those who come together in his name to work for justice. Paul VI recalled in *Populorum Progressio* that man cannot bring about his own progress unaided, because by himself he cannot establish an authentic humanism. Only if we are aware of our calling, as individuals and as a community, to be part of God's family as his sons and daughters, will we be able to generate a new vision and muster new energy in the service of a truly integral humanism. The greatest service to development, then, is a Christian humanism that enkindles charity and takes its lead from truth, accepting both as a lasting gift from

God. Openness to God makes us open towards our brothers and sisters and towards an understanding of life as a joyful task to be accomplished in a spirit of solidarity (*CV* 78)

APPENDIX 1: *TEN PRINCIPLES OF CATHOLIC SOCIAL TEACHING*

There have been many attempts to summarise the major themes of CST, and many different typologies. Because the purpose of *Faithful Citizens* is to link CST to community organising, I have summarised those elements of CST which speak most directly to those engaged in local politics as practised by London Citizens, ensuring that the key concepts of CST are included. What follows are ten distinctive principles of CST – key concepts which mark out CST as a school of thinking and reflection on social and political issues.

1 Dignity of the human person

Key to CST is the biblical idea of the intrinsic dignity of each person, created in the image and likeness of God. 'Intrinsic' means that dignity belongs to each person, and is not a concession of the law: it is a right to be vindicated, not a luxury to be begged for. It is not earned by achievements or bestowed by authorities other than God; nor is it dependent on a person's race, creed, colour, gender, sexual orientation or any other criterion on which societies throughout history have sought to divide people. There is a unique and sacred worth attached to each person by virtue of being created. Natural inequalities in talents exist among people but God has gifted all with equal dignity (*RN* 2). 'To consent to any treatment which is calculated to defeat the end and purpose of (man's) being', said Leo XIII, 'is beyond his right. He cannot give up his soul to servitude; for it is not man's own rights which are here in question, but the rights of God, most sacred and inviolable' (*RN* 40). When we argue for conditions to protect human dignity, or oppose conditions which undermine it, therefore, we are arguing not just for human rights but for God's.

The dignity of the human person has to be the starting point for every issue, not the needs of the market or the state. The commodification of human beings – seeing them firstly as factors in process of production, designed to maximise profit – is strongly opposed by CST, which constantly reminds people that the state and the market are there to serve human beings, not the other way round: human beings are not 'factors of production' like raw materials and capital. Pius IX lamented the way people were 'corrupted and degraded' in some factories, much like some modern offices and corporations, where exhausted men and women work long hours in front of computer screens, or in call centres and food-processing factories. Re-humanising these conditions is part of the mission of CST.

In the same way, the state and public authorities exist to serve people, not the other way round. 'The principle, "the state for the citizen, not the citizen for the state" is an old heritage of the Catholic tradition,' said Pope Pius XII.[1] As John XXIII pointed out: 'It is in keeping with their dignity as persons that human beings should take an active part in government' (*PT* 73).

In *Gaudium et Spes*, the bishops speak against 'whatever insults human dignity, such as subhuman living conditions, arbitrary imprisonment, deportation, slavery, prostitution, the selling of women and children; as well as disgraceful working conditions, where men are treated as mere tools for profit, rather than as free and responsible persons; all these things and others of their like are infamies indeed.' (*GS* 27). The Catholic bishops of England and Wales said in 1996: 'We believe each person possesses a basic dignity that comes from God, not from any human quality or accomplishment, not from race or gender, age or economic status. The test therefore of every institution or policy is whether it enhances or threatens human dignity and indeed human life itself' (*CG* 13).

2   The Common Good

The common good is ultimately the criterion for political action and judgement. Promoting or defending the interests of a group is all very well – especially if they are poor or vulnerable; but does justice for that group work to the good of society as a whole, even if another group opposes it? The common good is not what is good for most people, but the sum total of the social conditions that enable people to reach human fulfilment through the just ordering of society (*GS* 26). A good citizen seeks the common good by promoting that which promotes human fulfilment, namely peace, security, a sound juridical system, freedom of expression and religion, and the provision of essential services to all – food, housing, health, transport, education etc. (*CSDC* 166).

In this sense, the common good is strongly linked to social justice and the distribution of property and wealth. Noting how 'the distribution of created goods ... is labouring today under the gravest evils due to the huge disparity between the few exceedingly rich and the unnumbered propertyless,' Pius XI called for that distribution to be 'effectively called back to and brought into conformity with the norms of the common good, that is, social justice' (*QA* 197).

'Public authorities have the common good as their prime responsibility,' note the bishops of England and Wales. 'It implies that every individual, no matter how high or low, has a duty to share in promoting the welfare of the community as well as a right to benefit from that welfare.' Therefore, 'If any section of the population is in fact excluded from participation in the life of the community, even at a minimal level, then that is a contradiction to the concept of the common good and calls for rectification' (*CG* 70).

The common good is also, therefore, the criterion for state intervention. States have the right to interfere with the free market in order to protect the vulnerable. CST resists a minimalist, or 'laissez-faire' view of the state, just as it rejects an absorbing, centralising role. The key criterion for intervention here is the common good: where the state needs to intervene, it must do so not for the benefit of a particular group or class of people –although this is qualified by the *option for the poor*, for 'considerations of justice and equity can at times demand that those in power pay more attention to the weaker members of society, since these are at a disadvantage when it comes to defending their own rights and asserting their legitimate interests' (*PT* 56). Furthermore, the right and the duty of the state to intervene is qualified by the doctrine of *subsidiarity*, which requires that the state must do so to assist, not to absorb, organisations.

3   Priority of labour over capital

This principle flows from the dignity of the human person, and goes to the heart of the social crisis engendered by industrial capitalism. Much of *Rerum Novarum* is taken up with the question of labour – its purpose, worth, and dignity. – and this focus is taken up again 100 years later in John Paul II's commemorative encyclicals, *Laborem Exercens* and *Centesimus Annus*. Leo XIII was moved to pen *Rerum Novarum* because of the degradation he saw of people as subjects of work. With the demise of the guilds in the eighteenth century and the secularisation of laws, says Leo XIII, 'by degrees it has come to pass that workingmen have been given over, isolated and defenceless, to the callousness of employers and the greed of unrestrained competition ... so that a small number of very rich men have been able to lay upon the masses of the poor a yoke little better than slavery itself' (*RN* 2).

The alienation of workers from the fruit of their labour, so that they become little better than a mere 'factor in production', deeply troubled Leo XIII, as it did later popes, because the purpose of work – as set out in Genesis – is to serve an individual's humanity: the discipline and creativity involved in work are part of the expression of human dignity (*LE* 4–6). The danger of materialism and consumerism is that they reverse the order of Genesis: 'Man is treated as an instrument of production, whereas he ... ought to be treated as the effective subject of work and its true maker and creator' (*LE* 7).

People take priority over products and profits: the primary concern must be with the well-being of the workers, not the efficiency or profitability of the company (necessary although these are to its survival). The popes' protest against the commodification of human labour is a constant in CST – there are examples in virtually every encyclical.

Much of CST is taken up with the great question of modern capitalist society, the so-called conflict between capital and labour. In the CST analysis, capital and labour separated at the birth of industrialisation, when the confusion of the ends and means of labour took hold. CST urges a system capable of reconciling labour and capital, which has as its starting point 'the primacy of the person over things and of human labour over capital' (*LE* 13). Human beings are 'the source, the centre and the purpose of all socioeconomic life' (*GS* 63). Human labour is superior to other elements in economic life: economic activity detrimental to the worker is wrong (*GS* 67).

Labour and capital need each other (*QA* 53); historically, capital has claimed the products and the profits and left the bare minimum to labour (*QA* 54), although it is wrong for this injustice to be mirrored in another, unjust claim for all the profits and produce to belong to working people (*QA* 55). What is needed is a just distribution of wealth through the defence of the rights which flow from the dignity of labour: the right to work, the right to a just wage (enough to support a family), the right to education and leisure, the right to organise in labour unions, the duty of the state to intervene to protect the worker through social legislation, and so on (*RN* 5, 9, 48, 55, 62, 63, 69). Leo XIII and his successors are categoric that just because a worker signs a contract in which the worker agrees to work for a pitiful wage, that does not make the contract just. For 'if through necessity or fear of a worse evil the workman accept harsher conditions because an employer or contractor will afford him no better, he is made the victim of force and injustice' (*RN* 45).

The conditions of the workers which so appalled Leo XIII would be ameliorated by a better distribution of wealth and the spread of private ownership. 'Every effort, therefore, must be made that at least in future only a fair share of the fruits of production be permitted to accumulate in the hands of the wealthy, and that ample sufficiency be supplied to the workingmen' (*QA* 61).

4   The Universal Destination of Goods

'The law, therefore, should favour ownership,' said Leo XIII, 'and its policy should be to induce as many people as possible to become owners' (*RN* 46). While private ownership is a natural right – 'it is just and right that the results of labour should belong to him who has laboured' (*RN* 8) – it is a right curtailed by universal destination of all goods. This principle derives from God's will for humanity: 'God destined the earth and all it contains for all men and all peoples so that all created things would be shared fairly by all mankind under the guidance of justice tempered with charity' (*GS* 69).

CST accepts that inequalities are natural, but deplores the division of the world into haves and have-nots. It is not just a question of degree but of the way in which capital and property are concentrated in the hands of the few, giving the owners phenomenal power. Ever since Leo XIII lamented the way 'a small number of very rich men have been able to lay upon the teeming masses of the labouring poor a yoke little better than that of slavery itself', the popes have criticised a model of capitalist development which results in the few acquiring ever more while the majority suffer want.

A key criterion here is human need. The human person cannot do without the material goods that correspond to their primary needs, goods which are 'absolutely indispensable if he is to feed himself, grow, communicate, associate with others, and attain the highest purposes to which he is called' (*CSDC* 171). The universal destination of goods does not mean everything is at the disposal of everyone, but that society should be ordered as far as possible to enabling everyone to fulfil their basic needs.

CST strongly favours property and its spread. Where political regimes suppress private property, human liberty is extinguished; the right of ownership is therefore a matter of intrinsic liberty. But it does not follow that property should expand indefinitely in the hands of a few: 'the right to private property is subordinated to the right to common use, to the fact that goods are meant for everyone' (*LE* 14). From this follows the need, for example, to regulate the market to ensure the widest access to property.

A key means of spreading property in CST is the just wage, which is defined in CST as sufficient to allow a frugal person to save towards the cost of their own home. But in a society in which property is also the object of speculation, in which prices spiral to the point where even those on reasonable wages will never be able to afford to buy property in their lifetimes, more action may be called for: through affordable home schemes, for example, or by government intervention in the market.

The state cannot arbitrarily take away people's property: 'Man's natural right of possessing and transmitting property by inheritance must be kept intact and cannot be taken away by the State from man', said Pius XI (*QA* 49). 'However, when civil authority adjusts ownership to meet the needs of the public good it ... does not therefore abolish, but protects private ownership, and far from weakening the principle of private property, it gives it new strength.'

Pius XI preferred to put the principle of private property in terms of two dangers to be avoided. 'On the one hand, if the social and public aspect of ownership be denied or minimised, the logic consequence is "individualism", as it is called; on the other hand, the rejection or diminution of its private and individual character necessarily leads to some form of "collectivism" ' (*QA* 46).

5   Solidarity

Unlike many rationalist philosophies which see the human being as primarily an individual, naked before the state, CST starts from the person as a spiritual being, defined through interpersonal relations (*CV* 53). 'The more authentically he or she lives these relations, the more his or her own personal identity matures. It is not by isolation that man establishes his worth, but by placing himself in relation with others and with God. Hence these relations are of fundamental importance' (*CV* 53). The principle of solidarity springs from the social nature of the human person, and is both a social principle and a moral virtue (*CCC* 1939, 1942). As a social principle, it is strongly linked to justice, for it highlights the interdependence of all human beings, and is a commitment to seeking the good of one's neighbour, especially the most vulnerable. Solidarity, said John Paul II,

> is above all a question of interdependence, sensed as a system determining relationships in the contemporary world in its economic, cultural, political and religious elements, and accepted as a moral category. When interdependence becomes recognised in this

way, the correlative response as a moral and social attitude, as a 'virtue', is solidarity. This then is not a feeling of vague compassion or shallow distress at the misfortunes of so many people, both near and far. On the contrary it is a firm and persevering determination to commit oneself to the common good; that is to say, to the good of all and of each individual because we are all really responsible for all. (*SRS* 38)

Leo XIII and Pius XI deplored the way social fragmentation caused by free-market capitalism led first to individualism and then to class conflict, as people gathered on opposing sides of the capital–labour divide. They saw it as a priority to strengthen civil-society associations; or as Pius XI put it, 'It is necessary that social policy be directed towards the reestablishment of functional groups' (*QA*, 82). He earlier defines these (*QA*, 61) as trade or professional associations, as well as labour unions; but warned against the state establishing these, or creating state monopolies of unions and business associations, as happened in the contemporary fascist state. The demands of contemporary society – constantly to work, shop and spend, to 'have more' rather than 'be more' – diminishes our capacity for solidarity. Creating time for listening, either one-to-one or in gatherings and meetings, is a prerequisite for solidarity, for we must first know and hear each other, before we can properly engage with the world beyond the parish.

6   Subsidiarity

A key CST principle which strongly favours civil society, defined as 'the sum of the relationships between individuals and intermediate social groupings, which are the first relationships to arise and which come about thanks to the creative subjectivity of the citizen' (*CSDC* 185). In CST, the vitality of these 'mediating institutions' – family, parish, association, guild, fraternity, school, social club, citizen organisation etc. – are key to the health of a society, and need to be protected and fostered. Their existence precedes the state and they should not be absorbed or suppressed by it. Pius XI warns:

> Just as it is gravely wrong to take from individuals what they can accomplish by their own initiative and industry and give it to the community, so also it is an injustice and at the same time a grave evil and disturbance of right order to assign to a greater or higher association what lesser and subordinate organisations can do. For

every social activity ought of its very nature to furnish help to the
members of the body social, and never destroy or absorb them.
(*QA* 80)

Subsidiarity 'supports a dispersal of authority as close to the grass roots as
good government allows, and it prefers local over central decision-
making' (CG 52): decisions should be taken and action carried out as
close as possible to the people they affect.

Subsidiarity works both ways. Just as it is wrong for a higher organisation to subsume a lower one, it is also wrong for local, community
organisations (e.g. parishes) to fail to act to resolve problems on their
doorstep, expecting the state or the council to act. Subsidiarity requires
citizens to organise to compel those who have the power to act to do so, at
the level at which they are able to: it is a counterbalance to the principle of
solidarity, according to Benedict XVI, in that it prevents a paternalist
social assistance (*CV* 58). Indeed, 'Subsidiarity respects personal dignity
by recognising in the person a subject who is always capable of giving
something to others' (*CV* 57).

Subsidiarity rejects the message many have internalised: that we are
powerless to change the world around us. It is a principle which holds that
not only *can* power be exercised by active local organisations holding
politicians and employers accountable through assemblies, but that it
should be exercised in this way. Rather than wait for government to
introduce new legislation, local organisations should press for changes
locally, where they are – at the level at which change can be effected.

7   Participation

'Basic justice demands the establishment of minimum levels of participation in the life of the human community for all persons', say the US
bishops (*EJ* 77). Participation is one of the expressions of the principle of
subsidiarity. It means 'a series of activities by means of which the citizen,
either as an individual or in association with others, whether directly or
through representation, contributes to the cultural, economic, political
and social life of the civil community to which he belongs' (*CSDC* 189).

The common good – which citizens are obliged to work for – implies a
high degree of participation in decision-making. CST calls on all people
to be involved in the construction of a just society – to be 'active citizens'.
Individuals and families do not exist for the purpose of the state, but
vice-versa. But how are people to hold the state to account, and guide it
into serving the common good? Politicians must be answerable to voters

if they are to serve society, but who will hold them to account? Christians are called to be the leaven in society, and their participation is crucial at all levels to transform society from within, such that it reflects more the values of the Kingdom.

That means more than voting; it means acting to change the world around you. But it also means creating local mechanisms of participation. CST emphasises the need for forms of association, especially in the modern city, to overcome the alienation which lies behind much of the poverty and misery of contemporary society.

'One of the deepest forms of poverty a person can experience is isolation,' notes Benedict XVI. 'If we look closely at other kinds of poverty, including material forms, we see that they are born from isolation, from not being loved or from difficulties in being able to love' (*CV* 53). Paul VI speaks of the 'urgent need to remake at the level of the street, of the neighbourhood ... the social fabric whereby man may be able to develop the needs of his personality', and calls for community and parish associations and gatherings 'where the individual can escape from isolation and form new fraternal relationships' (*OA* 11).

To be 'public people' is not just a right, but a Christian obligation: to the extent we are able, this means that we are called to campaign and organise, building our power to affect the world around us and becoming 'citizens of change'. For some it means learning the arts of citizenship and leadership, to be able to bargain and negotiate with those who hold office. But whatever the means of participation, it is also important to promote at the same time the participation of the excluded, especially of the disenfranchised – giving a voice to the voiceless: 'The primary purpose of this special commitment to the poor is to enable them to become active participants in the life of society' (*EJ* 88).

8   Option for the poor

'This is an option, or a special form of primacy in the exercise of Christian charity, to which the whole tradition of the Church bears witness,' says Pope John Paul II.

> It affects the life of each Christian inasmuch as he or she seeks to imitate the life of Christ, but it applies equally to our social responsibilities and hence to our manner of living, and to the logical decisions to be made concerning the ownership and use of goods. Today, furthermore, given the worldwide dimension which the social question has assumed, this love of preference for the poor,

and the decisions which it inspires in us, cannot but embrace the immense multitudes of the hungry, the needy, the homeless, those without medical care and, above all, those without hope of a better future. It is impossible not to take account of the existence of these realities. To ignore them would mean becoming like the 'rich man' who pretended not to know the beggar Lazarus lying at his gate (cf. Lk 16:19–31)· (*SRS* 42)

The 'option for the poor' is a criterion for discerning how to judge a situation and act on it, one that CST believes should complement the others – common good, solidarity, subsidiarity, etc. – by making clear that the poor have a prior claim on our time and energy and commitment. This means, say the US bishops, 'The needs of the poor take priority over the desires of the rich; the rights of workers over the maximization of profits; the preservation of the environment over uncontrolled industrial expansion; the production to meet social needs over production for military purposes' (*EJ* 94). The poor and vulnerable, noted Leo XIII, have a special claim on the law, for they are deprived of other forms of protection (*RN* 30).

Bishops often note that the moral condition of a society can be judged in how it treats its most vulnerable members; and that one of the criterion in judging the fitness of a government is how well it responds to the needs of the poor through its public policies. The elderly, homeless, undocumented migrants, the unemployed, prisoners, the mentally ill – these are groups which are particularly vulnerable to being disenfranchised and exploited, and require the attention of both the state and civil society. The pursuit of their interests, and critique of the obstacles to their human development, will necessarily lead onto larger questions about public policies.

9 The gift of life and creation

'If you want peace, defend life,' said Pope Paul VI (World Day of Peace Message, 1977). God created life, and society must nurture it as a precious gift. Hence the stress in CST on family, education, human development, and the conditions needed for human life to flourish, and its call to work against all that shrinks and undermines those conditions: genocide, capital punishment, abortion, euthanasia, embryonic stem-cell research, assisted suicide, youth violence, drug gangs, and so on. The call is not just to combat these symptoms of the 'culture of death', but also to work towards changing the social injustices and circumstances which lead people to take part in them or tolerate them as normal. This might mean, for example, advocating on behalf of the elderly and single mothers, or working to create safer streets and leadership opportunities for young people. Building a culture of life is the most effective way to bring peace.

CST is not interested only in the spiritual life of people nor even the prolongation of biological life, but rather in the quality of life that reflects the designs of a provident God who desires the full development of every human being. CST recognises that destructive actions not only harm and injure the victims but also degrade and dehumanise those who inflict the destruction. Promoting a culture of life recognises this independence of all creatures and of creation itself.

It is an article of faith of CST that God created the earth to provide plentifully for humankind, and that food shortages and ecological disasters are the fruit of humankind's mishandling of nature. John Paul II notes:

> In his desire to have and to enjoy rather than to be and to grow, man consumes the resources of the earth and his own life in an excessive and disordered way. At the root of the senseless destruction of the natural environment lies an anthropological error, which unfortunately is widespread in our day. Man, who discovers his capacity to transform and in a certain sense create the world through his own work, forgets that this is always based on God's prior and original gift of the things that are. Man thinks that he can make arbitrary use of the earth, subjecting it without restraint to his will, as though the earth did not have its own requisites and a prior God-given purpose, which man can indeed develop but must not betray. Instead of carrying out his role as a co-operator with God in the work of creation, man sets himself up in place of God and thus ends up provoking a rebellion on the part of nature, which is more tyrannized than governed by him. (*CA* 37)

CST sees the ecological crisis as intimately connected with consumerism, which devours the resources of the earth in an excessive and disordered way. Modern productive methods have fuelled unprecedented consumption which are based more on a desire to have than to be. Only when a spirit of solidarity and restraint shapes our common quest for a better world will human beings realise the call to renew the earth as a faithful response to the God of Life.

10 Call to action

CST demands active participation. Paul VI said:

> Laymen [and women] should take up as their own proper task the renewal of the temporal order. If the role of the hierarchy is to teach and to interpret authentically the norms of morality to be followed in this matter, it belongs to the laity, without waiting passively for orders and directives, to take the initiatives freely and to infuse a Christian spirit into the mentality, customs, laws and structures of the community in which they live. Let each one examine himself, to see what he has done up to now, and what he ought to do. It is not enough to recall principles, state intentions, point to crying injustice and utter prophetic denunciations; these words will lack real weight unless they are accompanied for each individual by a livelier awareness of personal responsibility and by effective action.

This action, he said, would find an echo in others. 'For beneath an outward appearance of indifference, in the heart of every man there is a will to live in brotherhood and a thirst for justice and peace, which is to be expanded' (*OA* 48).

Analysis and discussion must not take the place of action. The enemy of action is a besetting modern sin identified by the desert fathers as *acedia* – a 'not caring', manifest in individualism and cynicism, workaholism and indifference.

CST is not a theory, but a tool for action. Looking back to *Rerum Novarum*, John Paul II recalled:

> After formulating principles and guidelines for the solution of the worker question, Pope Leo XIII made this incisive statement: Everyone should put his hand to the work which falls to his share, and that at once and straightway, lest the evil which is already so great become, through delay, absolutely beyond remedy, and he added, in regard to the Church, her cooperation will never be found lacking. (*CA* 56)

John Paul II added:

> Today more than ever, the Church is aware that her social message will gain credibility more immediately from the witness of actions than as a result of its internal logic and consistency. In the countries of the West, different forms of poverty are being experienced by

groups which live on the margins of society, by the elderly and the sick, by the victims of consumerism, and even more immediately by so many refugees and migrants. (*CA* 57)

APPENDIX 2: MAXIMS OF COMMUNITY ORGANISING

The universals of organising are principles and guidelines which under-pin the way BBOs secure victories. They show how community organis-ing is essentially pragmatic: it has an understanding of the way the world works – and the way, therefore, to secure change. There is no established canon of principles, but in London Citizens you'll regularly come across the following.

1   *Never do for others what they can do for themselves.* This 'iron rule' of organising fits well with CST's principle of subsidiarity. Community organising enables people to find their power and to practise it.

2   *All change comes about as a result of threat or pressure.* Whether in the market or the state, change is usually resisted, which is why pressure is necessary.

3   *You cannot negotiate until you have the power to compel negotiation.* To negotiate politically you must first be recognised. You gain recogni-tion by exercising power in some way.

4   *The action is in the reaction.* The purpose of action is to bring about change.

5   *Break down problems into issues.* An issue is effectively a slice of a problem that can be worked on. Choose something achievable to generate a sense of success.

6   *Power precedes programme.* In deciding what issue to work on, a citizens' organisation may choose something winnable and achiev-able, especially when starting out, in order to increase its power and gain recognition. Once these are achieved, the more important issues can be tackled.

7   *Action is to organisation as oxygen to the body.* The purpose of action is to build power. It gives a direct experience of politics. Too many actions can wear an organisation out; on the other hand, too much relationship-building without action will cause frustration.

8   *Personalise and polarise.* Find out who has the power to say 'yes' and target them.

9   *No permanent enemies, no permanent friends.* A corollary to the previous one. Once victory has been achieved, the personalised target can become a friend to the organisation, to be recognised and rewarded in assemblies. But the relationship shouldn't become so cosy that the friend cannot again be a target.

10 *Change means movement; movement means friction; friction means heat; heat means controversy & conflict.* Living with tension is key to success.

11 *Power is never conceded, only taken.* You don't beg; you ask (nicely). And if you don't get what you want, act.

12 *Make your enemy live up to their rule book.* The most effective actions hold up a mirror to an organisation's own values.

13 *The most effective action occurs within the experience of your people, and outside that of your target.* Christmas carols in an art gallery, serving teas and coffees outside an immigration centre – such irruptions of humanity in a soulless environment are testimony to a citizen organisation's values, and can be deeply disconcerting.

14 *What drags on for too long becomes a drag.* Short, clear campaigns and actions with clear beginnings and ends are best of all.

APPENDIX 3: LINKS, SOURCES AND FURTHER READING

The London Citizens (www.londoncitizens.org.uk) and Industrial Areas Foundation (www.industrialareasfoundation.org) websites are good places to explore the world of citizens' organisations. The Contextual Theology Centre (www.theology-centre.org/) in the East End, and Jellicoe Society (www.theology-centre.org/jellicoe.htm) websites are good places to reflect on community organising through the eyes of faith. In Milton Keynes, a new citizens' organisation (www.webjam.com/citizensmk2) is underway.

There are many videos at YouTube (www.youtube.com) of London Citizens assemblies and actions, including the moving 'A Christmas message to Mr Roy Evans'.

London Citizens campaigns – Living Wage, Our Homes Our London, CitySafe, Strangers into Citizens and Citizens for Sanctuary – have dedicated websites, accessible through its homepage (www.londoncitizens.org.uk), as does the Citizens Schools Alliance.

Books about community organising are mostly American: Michael Gecan, *Going Public* (Boston: Beacon Press, 2002) is the best introduction. Saul Alinksy's two classics, *Reveille for Radicals* (New York: Vintage Books, 1946) and *Rules for Radicals: A pragmatic primer for realistic radicals* (New York: Vintage Books, 1971) are still worth reading; a modern update is Ed Chambers, *Roots for Radicals: Organizing for power, action and justice* (New York: Continuum, 2004). A rambling but fascinating biography of Alinksy is Sanford D. Horwitz, *Let Them Call Me Rebel: Saul Alinsky, his life and legacy* (Knopf Doubleday, 2002). Two excellent surveys of the power of community organising in modern American politics are Richard L. Wood, *Faith in Action: Religion, race and democratic organizing in America* (University of Chicago Press, 2002) and Mark R. Warren, *Dry Bones Rattling: Community building to revitalize American democracy* (Princeton University Press, 2001).

Two British academics who write regularly on London Citizens and community organising are Maurice Glasman and Luke Bretherton. The latter's *Christianity and Contemporary Politics: The conditions and possibilities of faithful witness* (Oxford: Wiley-Blackwell, 2010) makes many references to London Citizens and the involvement of Christians in community organising, as does Jane Wills, *Global Cities at Work: New migrant divisions of labour* (London: Pluto Press 2009).

There are many books on Catholic social teaching. A classic accessible introduction is Edward P. De Berri and James E. Hug, *Catholic Social Teaching: Our best kept secret* (Maryknoll NY: Orbis Books, 4th edn, 2003). The compendious Kenneth R. Himes (ed.), *Modern Catholic Social Teaching: Commentaries and interpretations* (Washington DC: Georgetown University Press, 2004) brings together current experts to give detailed commentaries to accompany the encyclicals. *The Compendium of the Social Doctrine of the Church by the Pontifical Council for Justice and Peace* (London: Continuum, 2006) is a not always successful attempt to summarise the principal teachings.

The encyclicals themselves are available in various collected editions, or through the Vatican website (www.vatican.va). The website of the US Bishops' Conference (www.usccb.org/sdwp/projects/socialteaching/) offers a rich source of summaries, commentaries, quotes and ideas for putting CST into practice. Social documents of the English and Welsh bishops can be found at www.catholicchurch.org.uk/ccb/catholic_church/publications.

NOTES

Introduction

1 Peter Maurin, *Easy Essays* (Chicago 1977), p. 3.
2 Quoted in Susan R. Holman, *God Knows There's Need: Christian responses to poverty* (Oxford: Oxford University Press, 2009), p. 59.
3 Almost all of the $8m budget of the US bishops' Catholic Campaign for Human Development is spent on community organising efforts. See esp. Lawrence J Engel, 'The influence of Saul Alinsky on the Campaign for Human Development', *Theological Studies*, December 1998.
4 See http://www.dico-berlin.org/.
5 Confusingly, CitizensUK was known until recently as the 'Citizen Organising Foundation'. It was founded in 1988 by Neil Jameson, currently lead organiser of London Citizens, and executive director of CitizensUK.
6 For a brief history of TELCO, see Austen Ivereigh, 'Power to the People', *The Tablet*, 25 November 2006. For a recent profile of London Citizens, see Madeleine Bunting, 'Religions have the power to bring a passion for social justice to politics', *Guardian*, 12 January 2009.
7 Launch of the East London Communities Organisation (TELCO), 20 November 1996. Comments by Cardinal Hume, Archbishop of Westminster.
8 Among many books which tell the story of the dozens of broad-based community organisations in the US created by the Industrial Areas Foundation (IAF), three are particularly recommended as related to the Catholic experience: Michael Gecan, *Going Public* (Boston: Beacon Press, 2002); Ed Chambers, *Roots for Radicals: Organizing for power, action and justice* (New York: Continuum, 2004); and Richard L. Wood, *Faith in Action: Religion, race and democratic organizing in America* (Chicago: University of Chicago Press, 2002).
9 E.g. Wood, *Faith in action*. Also Mark R. Warren and Richard L. Wood, *Faith-Based Community Organizing: The state of the field. A Report of the findings of a national survey conducted by Interfaith Funders* (New York, 2001).
10 Two are quoted regularly in the following pages: Gecan, *Going Public*, and Chambers, *Roots for Radicals*.

Chapter 1: Catholic Social teaching: a deeper kind of politics

1 Catholic Bishops' Conference of England and Wales (CBCEW), *The Common Good* (1996), 15.
2 Kenneth R. Himes (ed.), *Modern Social Teaching: Commentaries and interpretations* (Washington DC: Georgetown University Press, 2004), pp. 2–5.
3 CBCEW, *The Common Good*, 24.
4 Stephen Pope, 'Natural law in Catholic social teachings', in Himes (ed.), *Modern Social Teaching*, p. 49.
5 G. Weigel, 'The free and virtuous society: Catholic social doctrine in the twenty-first century', address at Tyburn Convent, London, May 2004.

6   Introduction, in Himes (ed.), *Modern Social Teaching*, pp 5–6.

7   This shift discussed in Edward P. De Berri and James E. Hug, *Catholic Social Teaching: Our best kept secret* (Maryknoll NY: Orbis Books, 2003), p. 17.

Chapter 2: An introduction to community organising

1   Saul D. Alinsky, *Rules for Radicals: A pragmatic primer for realistic radicals* (New York: Vintage Books, 1971), p. 123.

2   Barack Obama, 'Why organize? Problems and promise in the inner city' in *After Alinsky: Community organizing in Illinois* (Springfield: University of Illinois Press, 1990).

3   A note on terms. We are using here the term 'community organising' to describe the method. The power alliances of institutions (mostly faith-based) which community organising builds – i.e. London Citizens – are referred to here as broad-based organisations (BBOs), whereas in the US they are known mainly as faith-based community organisations (FBCOs). The terms emphasise different aspects of organising, but in both cases they are mainly faith-based, while striving to include non-faith-based organisations.

4   There are four national networks which follow a faith-based community organising model in the US, as well as a number of smaller regional networks. According to a study made nearly ten years ago, there are about 4,000 institutions which belong to BBOs in the US; of these, about 3,500 (87.5 per cent) are religious congregations, the rest are unions, schools and other organisations. Most are very recent: the average founding date for FBCOs is 1991 (London Citizens was founded in 1996). See Mark R. Warren and Richard L. Wood, *Faith-Based Community Organizing: The state of the field. A report of the findings of a national survey conducted by Interfaith Funders* (New York, 2001).

5   M. Glasman, 'Abraham, Aristotle and Alinksy', paper given to Citizen Organising Foundation seminar, London Metropolitan University, 4 July 2007, p. 7.

6   See M. Glasman, *Unnecessary Suffering* (London: Verso, 1995), ch. 2.

7   This section is strongly indebted to Luke Bretherton, 'The origins of organising: a political and intellectual sketch', presented at the American Sociological Association Annual Conference, San Francisco, 7–8 August 2009, pp. 3–7. The paper is part of a broader, research project, sponsored by the Arts and Humanites Research Council, entitled 'Christianity, urban politics and pursuit of the common good through broad-based coalitions', due to be completed in 2011. For a theological analysis of broad-based community organising and the work of Saul Alinsky in particular, see also Luke Bretherton, *Christianity and Contemporary Politics* (Oxford: Wiley-Blackwell, 2010), ch. 2 .

8   Bretherton, 'The origins of organising', p. 6. Alinsky's famous texts are *Reveille for Radicals* (New York: Vintage Books, 1946) and *Rules for Radicals* (1971).

9   Glasman, 'Abraham, Aristotle and Alinsky', p. 4.

10 Madeleine Bunting, 'Religions have the power to bring a passion for social justice to politics', *Guardian*, 12 January 2009.

11 Quoted in Bretherton, 'The origins of organising', p. 14.

12 Saul D. Alinsky, *Reveille for Radicals* (New York: Vintage Books, 1969), pp 196–7.

13 Bretherton, 'The origins of organising', p. 15.

14 S. Horwitt, *Let Them Call Me Rebel: Saul Alinsky, his life and legacy* (New York: Vintage, 1989), pp. 167, 177, 190.

15 Horwitt, *Let Them Call Me Rebel*, p. 265.

16 Bretherton, 'The origins of organising', p. 18.

17 'While Alinsky's principles and the Church's social teachings were undoubtedly in agreement about the fundamental right people have to participate in decisions affecting their lives, they part ways in their attitude towards conflict. Alinsky welcomed it as necessary.' Allan Figueroa Deck, 'Commentary on *Popolorum Progressio*', in Kenneth R. Himes (ed.), *Modern Social Teaching: Commentaries and interpretations* (Washington DC: Georgetown University Press, 2004),p. 307. He goes on: 'Alinsky came upon this positive evaluation of conflict in the context of a democratic republic, the United States. Perhaps the inability of Pope Paul VI to deal more easily with the reality and the necessity of conflict in his approach to social justice issues is that he knows that the vast majority of the world's poor and powerless do not live in democratic republics. Consequently, they must be much more cautious than citizens, albeit poor and downtrodden, of democratic regimes.'

18 Marion K. Sanders, *The Professional Radical: Conversations with Saul Alinsky* (New York: Harper & Row, 1965).

19 Lawrence J. Engel, 'The influence of Saul Alinsky on the Campaign for Human Development', *Theological Studies* 59 (1988), pp. 636–61.

20 Mark R. Warren, *Dry Bones Rattling: Community building to revitatlize American democracy*, Princeton Studies in American Politics: Historial, International, and Comparative Perspectives (Princeton University Press), pp. 42–4.

21 Warren, *Dry Bones Rattling*, pp. 45–56. See also Michael Gecan, *Going Public* (Boston: Beacon Press, 2002), p. 9: 'While Alinsky had many gifts and strengths – among them the ability to make indelible impressions – he did not create organizations that endured. That was Chambers's critical contribution to the world of citizens organising and to America as a whole.'

22 Edward Chambers, *Roots for Radicals: Organizing for power, action and justice* (New York: Continuum, 2004), p. 64.

23 Bretherton, 'The origins of organising', p. 21.

24 Warren, *Dry Bones Rattling*, p. 58.

25 Edward Chambers, *Organising for Family and Congregation* (Franklin Square NY: Industrial Areas Foundation, 1978).

26 Bretherton, 'The origins of organising', p. 30.

27 Mark R Warren and Richard L. Wood, Faith-Based Community Organizing: The state of the field. A report of a national survey conducted by Interfaith Funders (New York, 2001), p. 6.

28 Gecan, *Going Public*, p. 4.

29 E. Cortes, 'Reflections on the Catholic tradition of family rights', in John A Coleman (ed.), One Hundred Years of Catholic social thought (MaryknollNY: Orbis Books, 1993), pp. 155–73, p. 161.

30 Warren, *Dry Bones Rattling*, p. 64.
31 E. Cortes, 'Reflections on the Catholic tradition of family rights', in John A Coleman (ed.), One Hundred Years of Catholic social thought (MaryknollNY: Orbis Books, 1993), pp. 155–73, p. 161.

Chapter 3: Civil society: stronger, together

1 Barack Obama, *Dreams From My Father: A story of race and inheritance* (New York: Times Books/Random House, 1995).
2 'Could safe havens prevent teenage stabbings?', *The Times*, 18 November 2009.
3 Jonathan Sacks, *Education, Values and Religion* (St Andrews: University of St Andrews, 1996).
4 Rodger Charles SJ, Christian *Social Witness and Teaching: The Catholic tradition from Genesius to Centesimus Annus* (Leominster: Gracewing/Fowler Wright Books, 1998), vol. 2, p. 25, quoted in S. Caldecott, *Catholic Social Teaching: A way in* (London: Catholic Truth Society, 2001), p. 34.
5 Quoted in *The Times*, 18 November 2009.
6 Beth Watts and Charlie Lloyd, 'What are today's social evils?' Available at www.socialevils.org.uk.
7 Madeleine Bunting, 'Religions have the power to bring a passion for social justice to politics', *Guardian* (12 January 2009).
8 Edward T. Chambers, *The Power of Relational Action* (Acta Publications, 2009), pp. 19–21.
9 Michael Gecan, *Going Public* (Boston: Beacon Press, 2002), pp. 139–40.
10 Edward T. Chambers, *The Power of Relational Action* (Chicago: ACTA Publications, 2009), pp. 19–21.
11 Michael Gecan, *Going Public* (Boston: Beacon Press, 2002), pp. 139–40.

Chapter 4: Assembling in solidarity

1 This section is indebted to an early draft by Catherine Howarth, first lead organiser of West London Citizens.
2 Sheldon S. Wolin, *The Presence of the Past: Essays on the State and the Constitution* (The Johns Hopkins University Press, 1990), p 139.
3 D. Littman, 'Another politics is possible', *Red Pepper*, 5 July 2008.
4 See Chapter 7 below for more details.
5 Austen Ivereigh, 'The free market in loans is inhumane', *Guardian*, 25 November 2009.
6 Christine Gudorf, 'Commentary on *Octogesima Adveniens*', in Kenneth R. Himes (ed.), *Modern Social Teaching: Commentaries and interpretations* (Washington DC: Georgetown University Press, 2004), p. 316.
7 Gudorf, 'Commentary', p. 323.

Chapter 5: A just wage is a living wage

1 'Tate workers stage wage protest', BBC Online news, 14 December 2007.
2 Sian Berry, 'Tate That', *New Statesman*, 17 December 2007.

3 Austen Ivereigh, 'Manning of the Barricades', *The Tablet*, 17 February 2007.

4 http://www.geog.qmul.ac.uk/livingwage/.

5 *Rooms for Change: Putting London hotels on track for the Olympics*, published by London Citizens and Unite, Central London hotel workers' branch, March 2009.

6 Taken from http://www.geog.qmul.ac.uk/livingwage/index.html.

7 Rachel Stevenson, 'The cleaner, the chairman, and the £2m differential', *Independent*, 31 May 2003.

8 'Barclays puts low pages beyond the pale', *Daily Telegraph*, 19 March 2004.

9 From Austen Ivereigh, 'A decent day's pay', *The Tablet*, 2 August 2008.

10 Valerie Voak's account from Frances Murphy, 'Strength in numbers', *Thinking Faith*, 31 October 2008.

11 Ian Tew, Head of Workplace at KPMG, 'Can capitalism deliver a Living Wage?', speech, 17 September 2008.

12 Jane Wills, 'The business case for the living wage: the story of the cleaning service at Queen Mary, University of London', January 2009.

13 Quoted in Ivereigh, 'A decent day's pay'.

14 See report by Andrew Bomford, 'Exploitation of workers at top hotels', BBC Online, 31 July 2009, http://news.bbc.co.uk/1/hi/programmes/newsnight/8171318.stm.

15 J. Wills, 'The Living wage', *Soundings: A journal of politics and culture 42* (2009), pp. 33–46, quotation from p. 38.

16 David Hencke, 'Children's minister voices opposition to London Living Wage: £7.45-an-hour recommendation for capital's workers branded "inflationary",' *Guardian*, 4 November 2008.

17 David Hencke, 'Gradgrind Ed Balls repents over London living wage', *Guardian*, 14 November 2008.

18 *Thinking Faith*, 18 August 2009, www.thinkingfaith.org.

Chapter 6: Dwelling in dignity

1 Michael Gecan, Going Public (Boston: Beacon Press, 2002), pp. 13–14.

2 Edward Chambers, *Roots for Radicals Radicals: Organizing for power, action and justice* (New York: Continuum, 2004), pp. 119–20.

3 These figures from London Citizens' own research, at http://www.londoncitizens.org.uk/affordablehomes/index.html.

4 http://www.londoncitizens.co.uk.

5 Pontifical Council for the Family, 'Charter of the Rights of the Family', 22 October 1983.

6 Pontifical Commission for Justice and Peace, 'What have you done to your homeless brother?' (27 December 1987), I.3.

6 'What have you done to your homeless brother?', III.2.

8 'What have you done to your homeless brother?', III.1.

9 'What have you done to your homeless brother?', III.3.

10 For an example of a successful CLT, consider the Burlington Community Land Trust in Virginia, one of the oldest in the US. After 19 years, the Burlington Trust

has more than 2,500 members living in houses run by co-operatives with total assets of $22 million. Between 1988 and 2002 the values of the homes increased by 62 per cent of Area Median Income, yet also became more, not less, affordable: three-quarters of former residents went on to buy homes in the open market.

11 Memorandum to the Prime Minister on Unaffordable Housing (May 2005), www.zk2.org.

12 Taken from Peter Ambrose, 'Discovering the meaning of "affordable housing",' April 2008.

13 Quoted in Janet Murray, 'I'd like somewhere to do my homework', *Guardian*, 16 December 2008.

14 Michael Lobo, Headmaster of St Mary's primary school, Battersea, speaking at the launch of the 'Housing Our Future' report, 15 December 2009.

15 Murray, 'I'd like somewhere to do my homework'.

16 Speaking at the launch of SLC's *Housing Our Future* report, 15 December 2009.

17 Peter Ambrose and Bernadette Farrell, *Housing Our Future: Report on an enquiry into the effects of overcrowding on children* (South London Citizens, December 2009). The commissioners were Prof. Peter Ambrose, Sir Michael Harris, Prof. Peter Mortimore and Robina Rafferty.

Chapter 7: Welcome, stranger

1 'Making everyone a winner', *Guardian*, 8 May 2007.

2 For a comprehensive survey of the presence of migrants in London's low-paid sector, see Jane Wills, 'Deregulation, migration and the new world of work', in J. Wills et al., Global Cities at Work: New migrant divisions of labour (Pluto Press, 2009), pp. 1–215.

3 Pope Pius XII, speaking on immigration in a radio address in 1951, on the fiftieth anniversary of *RerumNovarum*. Quoted in Pius XII, *Exsul Familia*, Title 1.

4 'Economic impact on the London and UK economy of an earned regularisation of irregular migrants to the UK', report by the LSE for GLA Economics. Download at http://www.london.gov.uk/mayor/business-economy/publications/ irregular-migrants.jsp.

5 Austen Ivereigh, 'Manning of the Barricades', *The Tablet*, 17 February 2007.

6 *Irregular Migration in the UK* (31 March 2006) was followed by an updated version (3 May 2009). Download at http://www.ippr.org.uk/publicationsandreports/ publication.asp?id=663.

7 United States Conference of Catholic Bishops, *Strangers No Longer* (2003), pp.34–8.

8 Catholic Bishops' Conference of England and Wales (USCCB), 'Mission of the Church to migrants in England and Wales' (2008), p. 3.

9 Joseph Carens, 'The case for amnesty: time erodes the state's right to deport', *Boston Review*, May/June 2009, at www.bostonreview.net/BR34.3/carens.php.

10 Statement by Cardinal Francis M. George, Archbishop of Chicago, on behalf of the USCCB, 18 June 2009.

11 There are a very large number of reports documenting the scale of destitution among refused asylum-seekers, e g Refugee Action, *Destitution Trap* (2006); Amnesty International UK, *Down and Out in London: The road to destitution for rejected asylum seekers* (2006); Centre for Social Justice, *Asylum Matters* (2008); and Independent Asylum Commission, *Safe Return: How to improve what happens when we refuse people sanctuary* (2008).

12 E.g. Madeleine Bunting, 'A modern-day slavery is flourishing in Britain, and we just avert our eyes', *Guardian*, 28 December 2006.

13 In fact, the Spanish regularisation there cost 12.7m euros; the year it was done, 2005, the additional income in social security payments and income tax amounted to 190m euros. Regularisation had not put an end to illegal immigration there – that was not its object – but it had certainly not led to more. Numbers of immigrants entering Spain between 2001 and 2004 was greater than after 2005, proving that regularisation reduces future illegal immigration by shrinking the shadow economy on which people-trafficking thrives. See Maria Alvarez, 'Popular, effective and no green-light effect: the Spanish regularisation of 2005', Strangers into Citizens briefing paper no. 3, at www.strangersintocitizens.org.uk.

14 Will Somerville, 'Can Obama fix immigration?', *Guardian*, 23 June 2009.

15 See *Hansard* for 20 June 2007.

16 'Lib Dems back amnesty plan for illegal immigrants', *Guardian*, 19 September 2007, at http://www.guardian.co.uk/politics/2007/sep/18/libdem2007.immigration.

17 Catholic Bishops' conference of England and Wales, 'Mission of the Church to Migrants in England and Wales' (April 2008).

18 'An amnesty for illegal immigrants? What staggering stupidity, Boris', *Daily Mail*, 24 November 2008.

19 'Immigration – time for an amnesty?' BBC *Panorama*, 9 March 2009.

20 'Economic impact on the London and UK economy of an earned regularisation of irregular migrants to the UK', report by the LSE for GLA Economics. Download at http://www.london.gov.uk/mayor/business-economy/publications/irregular-migrants.jsp.

21 Les Back, Bernadette Farrell and Eric Vandermaas, *A Humane Service for Global Citizens: Report on the South London Citizens Enquiry into Service Provision by the Immigration and Nationality Directorate at Lunar House* (2005).

22 See report by Iain Duncan-Smith's Centre for Social Justice, *Asylum Matters: Restoring Trust in the UK Asylum System* (December 2008).

23 'Asylum system "shameful for UK" ', BBC *News*, 27 March 2008.

24 See www.citizensforsanctuary.org.uk.

25 Jamie Doward, 'Anglican Santa barred from giving gifts to children at a detainee centre', *Observer*, 13 December 2009.

Appendix 1: Ten principles of Catholic social teaching

1 Quoted in Jean-Yves Calvez and Jacques Perrin, *The Church and Social Justice: The social teachingn of the popes from Leo XIII to Pius XII (1878–1958)* (Chicago: Henry Regnery, 1961), p. 13